Growing Up in British Malaya and Singapore

A Time of Fireflies and Wild Guavas

Maurice Baker

World Scientific

NEW JERSEY · LONDON · SINGAPORE · BEIJING · SHANGHAI · HONG KONG · TAIPEI · CHENNAI

Published by

World Scientific Publishing Co. Pte. Ltd.
5 Toh Tuck Link, Singapore 596224
USA office: 27 Warren Street, Suite 401-402, Hackensack, NJ 07601
UK office: 57 Shelton Street, Covent Garden, London WC2H 9HE

National Library Board, Singapore Cataloguing-in-Publication Data
Baker, Maurice, 1920–   , author.
    Growing up in British Malaya and Singapore : a time of fireflies and wild guavas / by
Maurice Baker. -- Singapore : World Scientific, 2014
        pages cm
    ISBN: 978-981-4623-77-3
    ISBN: 978-981-4623-78-0 (pbk)
    1. Baker, Maurice, 1920–   Childhood and youth. 2. Singapore -- Description and
travel. 3. Malaysia -- Description and travel. I. Title.
    LA2383.S552
    370. 92--dc23

                                        OCN881605469

British Library Cataloguing-in-Publication Data
A catalogue record for this book is available from the British Library.

Typeset by Stallion Press
Email: enquiries@stallionpress.com

Printed in Singapore

For my grandchildren Andrew,
Andrea, Leonard and Erin

Foreword

This book was conceived with one aim in mind, that is, to convey to younger readers, particularly in the lower levels of secondary school, what it was like to grow up before the Second World War, to live through the Japanese Occupation of both Malaysia and Singapore up to the return of the British. It is hoped that readers will feel and see a not so distant past recreated in vivid prose and rare photographs, and will be inculcated with a sense of national identity and pride.

I approached Maurice Baker to write his memoirs, knowing that he had lived through such tumultuous times and was willing to share the rich experiences of his youth with us. Through prose and poetry, his autobiography hopes to inspire more people to pursue this genre of writing, a genre which is relatively undeveloped.

Given the vast and accelerated change in every facet of our lives, we tend to focus narrowly on forging ahead, but perhaps should be reminded of a time before we called Singapore home; a simpler and more uncertain time. As we celebrate Singapore's 50th year of independence in 2015, I know that Baker's intriguing personal accounts of a vanished past will provide a valuable signpost for 21st century Singapore.

Robert Yeo

Preface

This is the story of my childhood and school-days in the Malay Peninsula (1920–1937) and my time in Raffles College, Singapore from 1938 to 1941. It is entitled *Growing Up in British Malaya and Singapore* as both countries were part of the British Empire then.

I have tried specially to depict what schools were like and generally what life was like for the young in those days. We led happy, carefree lives studying a little and playing a lot in a far less competitive environment than what prevails today. Most children usually walked or cycled to school. Bullock carts were perhaps more common than motor vehicles. The pace of life was placid and no one seemed in a hurry to get anywhere until the Japanese army stormed into our lives. We then moved fast enough to get out of the way of the brutal invaders!

I wish to thank Mr Robert Yeo of the National Institute of Education for urging me to write this book. I am indebted to Miss Jill Quah, Librarian of the National University of Singapore, for her invaluable assistance in making available all the facilities in the library. I am grateful to Mrs Daisy Hwang for typing the final version of this manuscript and Ms Susan Tan for typing an earlier draft. My thanks also go to Mr Wong Yeng Choon who was in school with me and who supplied the photographs of ACS Ipoh and Horley Hall; my sister Margaret for photographs of our parents, our brother and herself; and special thanks to my wife, Barbara, for her help and encouragement.

Life has changed so much in Singapore and Malaysia that I thought my recollections of the past might be of some interest to the youth of today and perhaps even to older readers.

MAURICE BAKER
Singapore

Contents

Chapter 1

Beginnings

I do not know the exact date of my birth and no one else knows either. This may sound strange to a Singaporean as I am sure everyone here, has a birth certificate. I have none. Why? This is because I was born in 1920 in a remote village in Kedah, a northern state in Malaysia or British Malaya, as it was then called. My English father was away on home leave in England and my Tamil mother, who was illiterate, knew nothing about registering the birth of a child. Anyway, records of births and deaths were not kept in villages and no one bothered about it. It was not until I had to go to school that my father obtained a Statutory Declaration from a magistrate fixing 24 March 1920 as the date of my birth. This was just a guess, but if correct, I fall under the birthsign Aries in the astrological calendar. According to my mother, I was delivered by a Malay *bidan* or midwife who cut the umbilical cord with a sharp bamboo knife which must have been germ free. It was 10 am on a bright, sunny day, she said.

I must tell you something about my unusual parents. My father was a brilliant but eccentric civil engineer who had won the top Professor's prize in engineering from King's College, London University in 1908 at the age of 20. As he was of an adventurous nature, he came to Malaya to work. He had to pass examinations in Malay and Tamil like other British civil servants. He picked up Malay easily but he had difficulty with Tamil which is much more complicated. I suspect one of the reasons he married a Tamil girl was to acquire proficiency in that language! Anyway my parents conversed in Malay, so my sister and I grew up speaking Malay and Tamil before we learned English in school.

My father, a well-built six-footer, kept a full reddish beard and a moustache which inevitably tasted his soup first! When he grew old, his beard and full head of long hair turned grey. He looked like a saint. He was living with me at the age of 70 in a two-storey university house in Lornie Road. I was then a lecturer in the university. One day we had a children's party to celebrate my son's fifth birthday. Lots of the neighbours' children were playing in the garden when one of them looked up and saw my bearded father standing in the balcony. The excited boy rushed indoors in amazement and shouted to his mother, "Mummy, Mummy, I have seen Jesus Christ! He is upstairs!" He was known wherever he lived as "the bearded tuan" or *tuan janggut*.

My father was a kind man who loved books — he was always reading at home after work — and animals. His first pet, I remember, was a monkey which was often perched on his shoulder and which regarded my sister and me as intruders. It bared its teeth to show its displeasure whenever we went near our father; so naturally we didn't care much for it either. In fact, we feared it somewhat. Many years later, when I was in Raffles College in the late 1930s, I often used to go to our Botanic Gardens where there were hundreds of monkeys who loved peanuts. They were more friendly than my father's pet. There are no more monkeys in our Botanic Gardens now.

My father was also fond of a tame mother elephant and her calf which used to pass our house in Kedah every morning. He bought bananas and sugar cane for them on a regular basis. As a result, the owner sometimes took me for an elephant ride. At first I was a little scared but soon got used to it. Years later, my father acquired a couple of ponies which were succeeded by a young female buffalo. My father went for his usual two-hour walk one evening. When he returned, we saw to our amazement that he was leading a half-grown buffalo. My mother was really taken aback and promptly questioned him. The dialogue went something like this in Malay:

Mother :   Whose animal is that?

Father :   It's a buffalo. I bought it for $25.

Mother :   *Alamak! Gilalah lu*! What are we to do with it? Where can you keep it?

Father :   In the garage. We'll take the car out and keep the buffalo there!

Mother :   So dirty *lah*! Who is going to look after it? It needs grass.

Father :   You! I know it needs grass. There's plenty of grass around. You can feed the buffalo.

Mother :   Nothing doing. Not me. The gardener will have to do it for extra pay. He's a Malay and Malays love buffaloes.

So the matter was settled. My mother came to like the animal so much eventually that she called it "Papatee" which in Tamil means butterfly. Imagine a buffalo being called a butterfly! All of us loved Papatee and she became a family pet. We took her to Cameron Highlands when my father retired there in 1935. My father used to ride her for charity shows and was pictured once in the *Straits Times* — a bearded white man in an outlandish Australian hat on the back of a buffalo! My schoolmates teased me endlessly about this. He believed that buffaloes were very docile and good-tempered despite their fearsome appearance and their call sounded more like the meowing of a cat than the loud "moo" of a cow. Singaporeans travelling in Malaysia, passing padi fields, may have seen Malay boys riding on the backs of buffaloes. There is a true story of how a buffalo saved a young boy, his master's son, from a tiger by facing the tiger with his formidable horns every time the tiger moved to pounce. The tiger gave up. Tigers almost always leap from the back and try to break the victim's neck.

Tigers were fairly common in Cameron Highlands in the 1930s. I myself once saw a beautiful fully-grown tiger crossing the Habu stream moving from one part of the jungle to another. I was standing at the window of my bungalow on a hill overlooking the stream very early in the morning when I was fortunate to catch a glimpse of one of nature's wonderful creations.

Maurice Baker's father in 1915 (left) and when he was in his seventies (above)

The Family's pet buffalo, Papatee's son, with Maurice Baker's father.

The English poet, William Blake, celebrated the beauty of the tiger in a poem, the first verse of which is as follows:

> Tiger, tiger, burning bright
> In the forests of the night,
> What immortal hand or eye
> Could frame thy fearful symmetry.

Although sometimes aged tigers in India turned into man-eaters as recorded by Jim Corbett in his *Man-eaters of Kumaon*, I know of only one instance when a tiger attacked a farmer in Cameron Highlands. The farmer defended himself with his *parang* and eventually hunters followed the tiger and shot it. The animal had a badly injured paw which had been caught in a trap. It could not hunt its usual prey of wild boar or deer, so it attacked a man as a last resort. The tiger is on the endangered species list and unless we human beings give these wonderful animals a chance to exist, future generations will be deprived of ever seeing them in their natural surroundings.

My father kept a cat and a dog which were the family pets; the cat often lying on my father's chest when he rested book in hand, in his rattan easy chair. Much as he loved his pets, I think he loved his books more. Every month parcels of books used to arrive from England so that he built up a large library on wide-ranging subjects including history, travel, comparative religions as well as the Victorian novels of Antony Trollope, Thomas Hardy, Dickens, Thackeray, Meredith and modern writers. His favourite novelist was Trollope whose complete works he acquired. He loved the comic novels of P G Wodehouse. He was more at home in the company of books than with friends as he was a teetotaller and a non-smoker who did not join any club. He spent all his evenings at home, never attending a party. It was rare for an Englishman to live as he did, but he was basically a shy and very private person.

My mother's favourite entertainment was to attend *bangsawan* performances in the evenings when a Malay drama group happened to be in town. The *bangsawan*, as I remember it, was usually a play about legendary kings and queens. The stage was bare except for the backdrops indicating a palace, street or jungle, but the actors and actresses wore gorgeous costumes. Years later, I was to discover the similarity between the staging of Elizabethan plays of the 16th century and the *bangsawan*. Shakespeare's great plays were also produced on bare stages with minimal props but the costumes were splendid. As a child, I was spellbound by the *bangsawan* which always began explosively with a loud firecracker as the curtains rose and the drama began. It is a pity that the traditional *bangsawan* is no longer popular. When I was in Raffles College in Singapore between 1938 and 1941, the amusement parks like the Great World in Kim Seng Road had theatres where the *bangsawan* as well as Chinese *wayangs* were often performed.

My mother had a large circle of friends who visited her frequently to gossip. As she could not read, this was her favourite pastime apart from buying jewellery and disciplining her children. She was very strict with me, my sister and later my brother, using the cane quite liberally to chastise us. My father never laid a finger on us. He disliked corporal punishment although the cane was more commonly wielded in homes and at school in those days than it is nowadays. He rescued us from my mother whenever he could. Unfortunately he was often away at work for weeks at a time as his drainage, irrigation and road-building duties required him to travel long distances far from the town. He was the first man to survey a route across the Malay Peninsula from Kuala Lumpur to Kuantan through the mountains and jungles. This is marked as "Baker's Trace" in old maps showing the plotting of the Maran–Karak highway from west to east of the Malay Peninsula. When the road was first opened, he was interviewed by the BBC on his experiences in the tropical jungle.

It was while he was on this job in 1926 that the great flood of that year deluged Malaya. It is well known that the East Coast is subject to annual flooding when the North-East Monsoon blows across the China Sea from October till March. But the great flood of 1926 was the worst ever and my family had to evacuate our bungalow, splashing through the floodwaters. My sister and I were carried on the shoulders of Tamil workers who waded through chest-high floodwaters to higher ground. There was water, water everywhere! To this day the rest-house in Kuala Lipis has the high watermark of the flood drawn near the ceiling. Pahang was the worst hit of the Malay states so we suffered most as we were living in Kuantan then. Rumours had it that my father and his team of workers were either drowned or eaten by tigers in the forest, but they survived on the mountains. The tigers were also stranded but they feasted on the deer, especially the *pelanduk* or mouse deer, which could not escape from them. It was weeks before the survey team, led by my father, emerged from the jungle. My father knew the jungle well and was so at home in it that even after retirement, he used to march off into the Cameron Highlands forest a whole day at a time. I accompanied him once — and only once — as climbing up damp, slippery slopes and contending with the leeches was too much for me. I kept out of sight whenever he planned to go trekking into the woods, pretending to be busy with my studies. I was then in school in Ipoh but spent my holidays in Camerons. This was in 1936 and 1937.

There was a beautiful shallow mountain stream called Sungei Habu flowing around the hill where our house is situated. I loved to hop from rock to rock as it sparkled in the morning sun and gurgled along — swiftly moving whirls of water. I enjoyed reading poetry, especially Shakespeare or John Donne, seated on a rock in midstream amidst the glittering ripples around my bare feet. Nowadays the stream is overgrown and heavily polluted by the farmers who dump their rubbish into it. The brook now struggles along, invisible to the eye, strangled by the undergrowth and in my imagination, it grumbles and grouses along instead of singing as it used to do in the 1930s.

When night fell, one was not disturbed by the harsh rumble of cars and buses and the street noises of the city. The jungle was not silent but the sound of the crickets competing with the cicadas, interrupted by the occasional hooting of the distant owl, was not unpleasant.

My mother, being a village girl, did not believe in doctors and hospitals. She was convinced the hospital was a death house. In fact, *kampung* folk only went to the hospital as a last resort when herbal cures failed and the local medicine man or *bomoh* declared that the evil spirit in possession of the patient was too powerful to be exorcised. When I fell ill with high fever at the age of five, my mother resorted to one *bomoh* after another. She even summoned a saffron-clad Siamese monk. I vaguely recall the monk muttering prayers while he held a lighted candle over a bronze vessel filled with water. The candle wax dripped, drop by drop, and floated on the water as I shivered and sweated with high fever. When the *bomoh's* magic failed to cure me, she rushed me to hospital where it was discovered that I was a victim of malaria. Daily doses of liquid quinine, pink in colour and horribly bitter in taste, brought me round gradually. My grandmother and mother spent most of the day in the hospital, a wooden structure with plenty of doors and windows for ventilation and far different from the modern air-conditioned Singapore hospitals. They fed me on chicken soup and rice porridge with dried salted fish which I loved. They did not trust the hospital food.

When I was discharged from the hospital, my mother did not give much credit to the doctors. She attributed the cure to her

Maurice Baker's father going for a ride on the son of his pet buffalo.

Maurice Baker's father (left) as a private in 1915 at age 27, and his mother (right).

prayers to one of the Indian gods. So she paid for an elaborate ceremonial feast where two goats, garlanded for the occasion, were sacrificed to the god. Each animal had its head struck off at a single blow. The blood flowed as each body fell twitching on the ground under a tall old raintree. I was upset but was assured that the goats died happy, being sacrificed to the healing god. I think it was the shock of the execution of the goats which imprinted the whole scene on my mind. I can recall the event vividly to this day.

Chapter 2

School

Nineteen twenty-six was the year I began schooling in Kuantan. I was scared at the prospect, possibly more than any other child of six, because my mother had frequently threatened that I would be taught to behave by rotan-wielding teachers. She did this to keep me out of mischief, especially to stop me from bullying my younger sister. My mother made bogeymen out of school teachers and Sikh policemen. (The Sikhs were tall and impressive, and even intimidating in their uniform, and I feared I would be arrested for being naughty. Before the Japanese Occupation (1942–1945), a great many policemen were Sikhs, both in Singapore and Malaya.) I had no specific image of a school teacher as a figure to fear but nevertheless I quailed at the thought of school. To me, it was a place of punishment for disobedient children. So I cried and struggled and had to be forcibly carried out of the car to the classroom on the first day! I suppose every child, even nowadays, clings to his mother's comforting hand on his first day in school. It was worse in my time as there were no kindergartens to get a boy or girl used to the idea of school. It was at the age of six at a proper school, that I, like the other children, learnt my ABC. We knew not a word of English, unlike children nowadays, most of whom can already read and write simple English in Primary 1.

The headmaster of the school was a kind, Indian gentleman who must have been used to frightened children crying on their first day. He calmed me down as he led me to my seat in the class. I remember his gentle ways but I do not remember my classmates at all. I don't recall learning anything either but I suppose I must have as the headmaster had written, "Maurice is a bright lad", on my leaving certificate. I had to leave after a year as my father was transferred to Mentakab, also in Pahang. I do not remember seeing a single cane in my first school. Teachers in other schools in Malaya and Singapore did believe in the liberal use of the rod as I was to discover during my schooldays.

Mentakab was my childhood paradise. There was no school building in that small town, so for a year I roamed around with a catapult, shooting — mostly unsuccessfully — at birds, or fishing with a bamboo rod or catching Siamese fighting fish in ponds. These colourful fish I kept in bottles. When two bottles, each with a fish, were placed side by side, the fish flared their colourful fins ready for battle. They had to be kept apart to prevent them from killing each other.

The games children played then were simple compared to the highly sophisticated games boys and girls indulge in nowadays. Marbles and top-spinning were popular among boys. The idea in playing marbles was to hit your opponents marble as far as possible using your middle finger, by bending it back with the marble as a projectile. Three shallow holes were made in the ground about four feet apart. Each competitor had to get his marble into each of the holes and whoever scored ten holes was the winner. The loser had to expose his knuckles at the end of the third hole while the winner aimed the marble, again using his middle finger, to hit the loser's knuckles. This could be a little painful. Top-spinning was a common sport and every lad had his favourite top which could be bought in toy shops. The idea was to outspin your opponent — to keep your top moving longer than your opponent's. A variation in the game was to hit a moving top with your own. Players took turns doing this. One had to be skilful and accurate to score a hit.

We used to carry empty matchboxes to keep fighting spiders which we caught in hedges and bushes which were common in our day. The top of the matchbox was the battlefield. The fight was usually very brief. The defeated spider was released and the winner stayed in the box to fight again another day.

Kite-flying was as popular then as it is now, although our kites were simple structures, which were homemade, on a fine bamboo frame. Kites could be bought at 10 cents each. The strings were sometimes smeared with crushed glass mixed with resin to sever an "enemy" kite. But more often, it was sheer joy just watching the kite soaring in the wind, high in the sky.

Such were our simple pleasures.

Mentakab was surrounded by forests and was really more of a village than a town. You could call it a "one-horse town". Though there were multitudes of insects including mosquitoes to make life irritatingly itchy, there were also the mysterious and beautiful fireflies to light up the night. I recall seeing entire trees illuminated, all aglitter and aglow — almost like Orchard Road at Christmas. The night twinkled with a million eyes to fill the air with loveliness. I did not know then that the twinkling lights were mating signals of the female fireflies to the male fireflies to come and get them! The males too winked their willingness to respond.

By day there were the fiercer dragonflies, multicoloured miniature helicopters flitting about hunting for food, especially over weed-covered ponds. Some of these ponds bred lotus plants and pretty water lilies. The lotus pods were delicious to eat. I often gathered them and took them home to enjoy them. Dragonflies, which are among the fastest flying insects, lay their eggs in the water. Here the eggs hatch and the nymphs grow till they are ready to take to the air. This is perhaps why dragonflies frequent ponds overgrown with weeds, hunting for mosquitoes and other small insects. I found such ponds even in Switzerland in the coniferous woods which the Swiss preserve near their towns. Small scattered woodlands are the lungs of a city, just like our Botanic Gardens.

One thing about living near jungles is the presence of snakes, which at times found the bathroom cooler for a snooze on hot, steamy days. I recall several incidents when these unwelcome visitors panicked my mother into running out of the house screaming for help! One of the famous British civil servants, Sir Frank Swettenham, who loved to sleep with his doors and windows open, mentions in his book *Unaddressed Letters* how his Chinese cook complained that open doors brought in "plenty long snake, plenty short snake" into the house. Sir Frank reluctantly had to shut his doors and windows. Of course most snakes are non-poisonous but one could not take a chance with cobras, vipers and the banded krait. Snakes, are not aggressive by nature and even the poisonous hamadryad or king cobra is falsely believed to be so. A motorcyclist in Cameron Highlands once reported being chased by one for a considerable distance but I have my doubts about this incident. The hamadryad eats other snakes. M W F Tweedie in his books *Poisonous Animals of Malaysia,* refutes the claim that the king cobra attacks without provocation. Tweedie pointed out that in 1951 a hamadryad was found in the Island Golf Course in Singapore. It was large and mistaken for a python. It was caught by its tail but it did not bite. It was obviously not aggressive. Snakes tend to slither away from man's presence unless threatened or stepped on by mistake. The snake is a much maligned reptile whose ferocity is highly exaggerated.

My only encounter with a snake was in Cameron Highlands. As I was coming down the staircase of my house, our pet cat shot past me like a bullet. I looked down to see a big snake at least five or six feet long after the cat. The snake upon sighting me immediately swung round and glided away swiftly. My father and I searched the grounds but in vain. It had disappeared in the undergrowth.

When I was in Kuala Lumpur as Singapore's High Commissioner, I stayed in the official residence which was close to the Royal Selangor Golf Club. I saw several snakes, especially cobras which came into the garden looking for frogs. Once my dog Max confronted an angry cobra which raised its hooded head and spat poison at him. Fortunately the poison missed his eyes and a thorough washing of his face made it evident that he was unharmed. We made so much noise that the snake slid away into the golf course. The High Commission's gardener told me once that he had a good relationship with cobras which he often found resting in the hedge. "I tell them I'll leave them alone if they leave me alone!" he said. He has never had a confrontation with a snake in his twenty years as a gardener and did not believe in killing any. Max, however, obviously disliked snakes. Once he brought a cobra he had killed into the kitchen and dropped it at the feet of Alicia, the maid. She certainly did not appreciate his gift! Most snakes, however, are harmless.

It was in Mentakab that I learnt to ride a bicycle. Is there any excitement to excel the thrill of one's first bike? It was a Christmas present, the cycle with its shining spokes and handle bar complete with a bell or *loceng* — pure music! Then followed my attempts to mount the wobbling monster with the help of my father holding on! I would make a little move forward by pressing the pedals but the cycle seemed determined to shake me off like a bucking horse. I struggled to balance on the slippery saddle and in a day or two came the miraculous moment when I stayed on the seat, holding my breath, pedalling faster and faster. In a panic I realised I didn't know how to stop or get off. Sheer fright of falling gripped me. My cycle carried me fast and straight into a newly cleared patch of jungle at a bend on the downhill road. I shut my eyes and crashed. When I got up I was more concerned for my new cycle than my bleeding knee. After a proper scolding, my knee was attended to. My mother's sovereign remedy for all cuts and wounds was an application of cobwebs, lime and herbs. Sure enough the wound healed though I bear the scar to this day! Soon I rode again, more in control and with greater confidence. The bicycle had found its master!

What fun it was to cycle along a quiet road. I imagined I was riding at breakneck speed, overtaking every vehicle on the road, even cars! Fantasy is a common characteristic of childhood which makes life exciting. Every child is his own hero winning races, climbing mountains, swimming lakes and overcoming endless obstacles. He or she always reaches the winning post first, which cannot happen in real life of course. A child's fantasy world compensates for the disappointments of life.

Occasionally when my parents had to travel by car, we children had a lot of fun. My mother always prepared for the journey by bringing tiffin carriers of rice, curry and vegetables, no matter how short the distance we had to travel. My father, who was nervous about speed, invariably instructed the driver to *perlahan-lahan* — go slower. Sometimes he would stop the car at a bridge and lecture us as to how badly that particular one was built — it was too big or too small. He would also stop at sharp bends on the road to show us how much better the road could have been built. My mother seized on such opportunities to locate a tree under which we could have a picnic with the food she had brought. A journey with my parents was at times hilarious!

By the end of the year, I heard the bad news that education had caught up with Mentakab. An attap-roofed shed of a school for two primary classes for boys had been built. It had one teacher, an Englishman. I was in Primary 2 but as I had forgotten what little I had learnt in Kuantan, I was lost in class and last in class. But my humiliation was brief as my father was transferred again, this time to Perak where we were given a government bungalow in Ipoh. This town is named after a tree from which the *Orang Asli* or aborigines extract the poison for their blowpipes.

While in Mentakab, we didn't have a car and as I was not allowed to ride my cycle, I had to walk to school and back — about three miles in all. Not too great a distance for an active lad, After school I was off bird-hunting with an Indian lad — a cowherd, taller, thinner and a little older than I was. His large limpid eyes lit up his face with honesty, but alas, he charged me five cents (half my daily pocket money) for the privilege of accompanying him into the forest with his cows! The five cents, he claimed, was to protect me from tigers which had once killed and devoured a cow in that area.

"This big, big tiger very fierce, you know," he said, opening his eyes wide and adding, "he eat you up! He eat up a cow too, three years ago. I save you. Five cents only."

I was never sure as to how I was to be protected if a tiger did appear but I never doubted the courage of my bodyguard. I was naive. Perhaps that smart lad grew up to own a whole herd of cows or a dairy farm. The romp in the woods was fun, especially as we stalked the birds beside a stream while the cows grazed peacefully on the foothills. But it wasn't the thrill of chasing birds alone. Sometimes we spotted wild guavas or *jambu*. The *jambu* trees are ubiquitous, the seeds being scattered by birds. Why is it that a fruit growing wild or stolen from someone's orchard always tastes so much sweeter to a young boy?

I don't think I was always naive. My sister claims that I was quite cunning, for instance when I was tempted by a home-made cake. My father was very fond of chocolates, sweets and cakes — like most non-smokers. He never ate eggs in any form — half-boiled, poached, scrambled or fried — but he loved cakes. Our Hainanese cook, Ah Meng, was an expert at baking rich butter cakes whose aroma alone made my mouth water. On one occasion when the cake had been placed in the pantry two hours before teatime, I just couldn't bear to wait. But how was I to taste it without being caught? According to my sister, I solved it in this way. I sliced off a bit from the bottom of the cake so that it would be difficult for anyone to discover that the cake had grown slightly shorter. My sister who caught me in the act did not betray me, so I got away with it. She thought my trick typical of a sly character like me but I prefer to think of it as a clever solution to a problem!

It was while we were in Mentakab that my grandmother died in the Bentong hospital. She was only in her fifties and I remember her as a loving and talkative lady who bossed my rather frail maternal grandfather. He, however, outlived her by twenty years. The Hindu rites at her funeral, noisy with lamentations and loud beating of drums all the way to the cemetery, echoed for a long time in my memory. Ritual and ceremony at funerals help to distract the bereaved family from their grief at their irreparable sense of loss. I loved my grandma and missed her for she was a kind and caring woman.

Ipoh

My father's government bungalow in Jalan Bendahara in Ipoh was situated among rubber estates three or four miles from town. It had a large compound where my chickens could roam — scratching for worms and hunting for insects. I kept chickens as pets and loved to watch a mother hen surrounded by a dozen fluffy chicks responding to her clucking whenever she scratched around and found a juicy worm or insect for them. Any observer will learn to recognise the varying calls of a hen to her chicks: the warning of danger of a hawk overhead which sends the chicks scampering into the grass to hide; the inviting "cluck-cluck" to share a delicious morsel; or an angry warning with fluffed up feathers to dissuade wooing roosters. The great Austrian naturalist Konrad Lorenz in his book, *King Solomon's Ring*, reveals how birds "talk" to each other. It was exciting too, watching chicks pecking their way out of the eggs from under their brooding mother on the 21st day. Occasionally I was able to help a damp weaker chick out of her shell. Mother hens are very protective of their young and keep them warm under their wings at night. In the New Testament there is a moving passage in St Luke, when Jesus, looking at Jerusalem, wished the inhabitants would have responded better to him. He would have gathered them "even as a hen gathers her brood under her wings".

One thing about the behaviour of chickens puzzled me. I could not understand why the roosters often chased the hens and jumped on them. I regarded this as a case of bullying and often tried to rescue the hens! This caused immense amusement to my mother and her cronies. No one bothered to explain the processes of nature — or what is popularly called "the birds and the bees" — to me. I stayed innocent for a long time. As I said before, I was a naive lad at times.

Despite what I thought was the ill-natured behaviour of the roosters, I admired their colourful feathers, their splendid red combs and wattles, and their proud stance generally. The domestic cockerels descended from the wild jungle fowls are like the flamboyant pheasants in their multicoloured feathers. They looked as if they were in fancy dress! I think birds are among the most beautiful living creatures, especially in their natural surroundings pursuing insects or singing, as the poet John Keats said, "with full-throated ease". Nowadays in my small garden in Cassia Drive, Singapore, I feed the ring-necked doves and numerous sparrows with unpolished rice, the mynahs and the yellow-vented bulbuls

The government bungalow in Jalan Bendahara, Ipoh,
where Maurice Baker lived in 1929 and 1930.

Maurice Baker with his pet chickens in the compound
of the government bungalow in Jalan Bendahara.

with papayas and bananas. They love bread too. The beautiful golden and black-naped orioles are ever on the lookout for fruit. Their call is melodious but I think the small bulbuls are our best singers — our nightingales.

I made a special pet of a young cockerel who matured into a big bird, resplendent in his red and gold feathers iridescent in the sun. He knew me well and used to follow me around. I could pick him up and carry him about. He loved to feed from my hand. Unfortunately he got into the habit of ambushing the women in the house, often pecking their legs. He was a naturally aggressive rooster and so the maids, as well as my mother, disliked him. They complained frequently and even displayed the reddish-blue marks made by his beak on their legs. I paid no attention to their protests. What else could I do? There was no way I could train the bird to refrain from attacking women; curiously enough he ignored the men. He must have been a misogynist! But the poor fellow paid dearly for his pranks.

One day when I returned from school I missed him. He was usually around to greet me. I searched everywhere but in vain. Everyone was silent but eventually my mother said that perhaps a wild cat or *musang* might have got him. I believed her as *musangs* were common in the county and, like foxes, often did steal chickens. I was really sad over the loss of a friend. I wept. In the evening, one of the maids whispered to me to look into the cooking pot. I rushed into the kitchen and sure enough, the claypot was full of chicken curry. In a fury I picked up the pot and smashed it in the drain, spilling all the contents. It took me a long time to forgive my mother for her thoughtless act. She did not realise how much I cared for the rooster and how deeply I would suffer his loss.

I used to rear some ducklings too, digging earthworms for them in the evenings after school. Ducklings love earthworms and gobble them up as a special treat. I noticed that ducks are much more gregarious than chickens and appear to love each other's company. They move around in a flock whereas chickens are distinctly individualistic and self-centred like human beings. They fight and establish a pecking order both among cocks and hens. This can be observed on any free-range farm, which unfortunately cannot be found in Singapore. Farmyards are common in Malaysia although even there chickens are commercially raised in limited spaces and never have a chance to run around scratching in the soil for worms or chasing an insect in the sun. Ducks appear to get along better than chickens with each other, often following the leader to a pond. They love water so they cannot be reared in cages like the poor chickens. The pullets, which are kept in small cages for their eggs, do not have enough space even to flap their wings but eggs produced under these conditions are cheap; cruelly produced but cheap. Free-range eggs cost more and they are available in Europe and Malaysia. In Europe, there is some pressure on chicken farmers from animal protection organisations to produce the more expensive free-range chickens and eggs. I hope one day people will become more sensitive to the needs of fellow creatures who share the world with us as can be seen in Gerald Durrell's many interesting and humorous books on animal behaviour.

The last Friday of every month was what one would call a "clean-out" day. It was a day we dreaded. My sister, brother and I were lined up and forced to swallow a tablespoonful of castor oil, a nauseous, smelly purgative which certainly did its job thoroughly. I am sure our insides were washed out "whiter than white" which is the effect claimed for modern detergents. We were forced to fast the whole day and only allowed rice gruel or *bubur* in the evening. Believe it or not, castor oil was the popular laxative recommended by doctors in those days. The first time I faced castor oil, I ran, but I was caught and the thick oil was forced down my reluctant throat. Later I resigned myself to the inevitable every last Friday of the month. It was only when I became a boarder in Horley Hall that I escaped this oily horror! Children nowadays no longer suffer from the castor oil treatment. How lucky they are! Instead of castor oil, they are brought up on sugar-coated vitamin pills. We knew nothing of vitamins but we were given regular doses of cod-liver oil to build up our resistance to tuberculosis. I was also given a more pleasant health supplement called "Radiomalt" which tasted like melted toffee. I liked it so much that it had to be kept on a high shelf out of my reach so that I wouldn't gobble it up like chocolate. My mother made sure that there was no ladder in sight. I did try standing on a chair but no matter how hard I stretched, I just could not reach the bottle. Some of my father's books piled on the chair brought me precariously nearer the target but I tumbled. No Radiomalt, but I got the cane instead from my mother. It was no sugar-cane either.

Chapter 3

The Anglo-Chinese School, Ipoh

The pleasant playtime with chickens and ducks intermingled with fishing, catapult hunting and kite-flying were to come to an end when my father decided I should be put into a boarding school. I was then in the afternoon session of the Anglo-Chinese School in Ipoh in 1930 which admitted overaged boys, as well as those who were backward in their studies. It was called the "continuation school". The brighter children attended the morning school.

The Anglo-Chinese School run by the Methodist Mission stands splendidly on a hill overlooking Lahat Road. It is architecturally imaginative and a far more inspiring building than the purely functional school buildings one sees nowadays. Why my father chose this school rather than the government school or St Michael's, a well-known Catholic School in Ipoh, I do not know. But for me it turned out to be a happy choice. To this day I look back with nostalgia to my years in the ACS and its devoted band of teachers.

My first months were a total misery. I think I was placed in Standard I or Primary 3 which was taught by a young Mr Leong who wielded his cane with relish. My schooling had been so interrupted that I could not spell or do the simplest sums. My dictation pieces had more mistakes than correct words and when marked it became a sheer of red ink. At first I could not even distinguish between "his" and "is". English was foreign to me despite having an English father who, as I said earlier, spoke Malay to me. In school we were forbidden to use any language except English which perhaps accounted for the higher standard of English spoken and written during the old days in Malaya and Singapore. There was no one to help me with my arithmetic homework so I often copied the answers from classmates. Mr Leong inspired fear and I longed for the end of the school day. He never understood why my work was so poor and caned me often. It didn't help and I failed miserably at the end of the year as I had entered the class in mid-year. So I was kept back in the same class the following year. Only those who passed were promoted. There was no "automatic" promotion in those days. The failures remained behind for another year.

The following year, all of a sudden, everything clicked in my studies just like the moment of mastery over the bicycle. I do not recall concentrating on my books and I certainly had no private tuition. But I used to pray in the rickshaw on the way to school, "Lord," I pleaded, "help me with my examinations and I promise to be a good boy!" I have no rational explanation of what happened but my class work improved rapidly and to the astonishment of Mr Leong, I stood second in class at the end of the first term. He congratulated me on having worked very hard, imagining that I had toiled, sweated and stayed up late with my books! I didn't disillusion him! I had begun reading from my father's large library and my first book on his recommendation was R M Ballantyne's *The Coral Island,* an exciting adventure story of the three boys, Jack, Peterkin and Ralph marooned on an island. I lost myself too with those lads on that island and enjoyed, suffered, endured and came triumphantly through every incident that happened to them. Subsequently I read other books by the same author but I liked none as much as I liked *The Coral Island,* my first love among books. To this day I am unable to explain my leap from being a dud to being among the top in every class in my school. It was a minor miracle.

The following year, I moved up a class for a term but was then transferred to the morning school along with the late Goon Sek Mun, my closest friend in school, who was later to become a distinguished Professor of Gynaecology & Obstetrics in Singapore. We were so happy in class with our wonderful teacher Mr Rasiah who was so kind and understanding. He encouraged us to do our best without ever threatening us with a cane — he did not have one and never needed it — that we were reluctant to leave him for the morning session. However the principal, Dr Proebstel, a big left-handed American with a crewcut, came down to see us. He had got to know us as he set and marked all compositions throughout the school, which meant marking four to five hundred scripts! This shows you how dedicated our teachers were in ACS. He had a peculiar system of marking. In theory, each candidate could score 200 marks for a perfect composition. He subtracted 25 marks for every comma left out and 50 marks for every full-stop missed. Ten marks were deducted for spelling mistakes and 20 for grammatical errors. He appeared personally in class to return the scripts. Only two of us passed in our class, the top mark being 55 which meant that 90 marks had been deducted from 200 leaving 110 marks. This was then divided by two. Many pupils owed him a lot of marks, the worst owing him 600 marks. Dr Proebstel said that he would be back the next term to collect the debts. Both Goon and I passed so we were simply ordered to report ourselves to the morning school the following week. This we did.

Our new timetable included Reading, Writing, Dictation and Spelling, Literature and Arithmetic. There was also an art class once a week. The writing lessons were conducted by an American lady who insisted on our using a 'G' nib on a penholder and carrying a bottle of ink. No fountain pens were allowed. We were individually taught how to shape each letter in copying out paragraphs from a book as neatly as possible. The result of this intensive training was that most of us learnt to write legibly. The reading lessons were taken by the class teacher. Pupils were called upon at random to stand up and read a paragraph or two loudly to the class with the teacher correcting pronunciation. Dictation meant writing as the teacher read out a passage from a textbook. We were required to spell ten words at the end of the dictation passage. For composition, a story was read out twice by the teacher. We had to listen carefully without taking any notes and then reproduce the passage from memory. It was only in the higher forms that we were taught how to write essays. Arithmetic was a torture as we had to do sums dealing with the old English system of pounds, shillings and pence, now mercifully outmoded and replaced by sensible metric system. We had also to master yards, feet and inches which are not in use in Singapore anymore. On top of all this we had to learn that four *cupak* made a *gantang* of rice and so on. Algebra and geometry were not taught till Standard VII when we were 13 or 14 years old. You can see how different our studies were from the school curriculum nowadays.

Horley Hall boarders with its principal, Mr R Kesselring, in the
middle. Maurice Baker is next to him on the right. The boarding
school, which is still used today, is in the background (1935).

The Anglo-Chinese School in Lahat Road, Ipoh, today as in the 1930s.

Chapter 4

Boarding School

It was from this new class that I had to join Horley Hall. One morning my heart sank when the Reverend Ralph Kesselring appeared in class and called out my name. He was a gifted American missionary teacher in his 20's, who, I was to discover, was a caring boarding master as well as a stimulating teacher of Literature and Mathematics (especially Algebra which thrilled him but not me). He infected us with his enthusiasm and won us with his understanding and patience. He ran the boarding school of about 40 of us in good order and kept us happy — no mean accomplishment as some of the boarders were potential hooligans sent there by exasperated parents! All this I was to find out later. Fearful and utterly miserable, I arrived in Horley Hall the next day with my books and a small bag of clothes. I was given an iron bedstead and mattress in dormitory "A" — there were four dormitories in all. There were ten beds in every dormitory. Over each bed was a locker on the wall for our personal effects. One of the senior boys, John Ritchie who was later to become a police commissioner in Malaysia, was told to look after me.

Horley Hall, named after the Methodist missionary and founder of the Anglo-Chinese School, still exists today. It is a large double-storey wooden building fronted by the school football field, close to the Malaysian railway lines beyond which lies a Christian cemetery. This graveyard was visible through the windows facing the field which remained open day and night for ventilation as air-conditioning was unheard of in the 1930s. In fact there was no need at that time for air-conditioners as the presence of many trees in the immediate vicinity as well as the forests not too far away kept the environment cool.

The nearness of the cemetery was disturbing to imaginative young minds brought up on tales of ghosts. My mother was a great believer in evil sprits and kept all doors and windows at home firmly closed more to keep out ghosts than thieves! She even had the curious belief that one's own soul tended to leave the body in the dead of night in search of adventure. She kept the curry pots closed tight in case the soul, in search of tasty morsel, left the body too long! Brought up with such superstitious beliefs, I was naturally uneasy about the proximity of the graves to Horley Hall. Every once in a while, a boy would claim to have seen mysterious blue lights flickering over the tombstones. Others claimed to have struggled with a ghost squatting on their chests, choking them!

Miserable at having to leave home, fearful of the future in the boarding school, I spent the first night in tears. It was a night of the full moon. From my bed I could see a huge raintree whose branches seemed like the tentacles of an octopus reaching out for me. The night bristled with menace in my overwrought imagination. I tossed and turned waiting for the dawn to dispel my fears.

6 am. The prefect rang the morning bell loud and clear. Discipline began for me for the first time in my life. It was one mad rush for the 40 of us to the outdoor bucket toilets (no flush toilets in those days), then the cold morning shower bath before

dressing for the communal breakfast of toasted bread and butter, with eggs and tea. Meals began with a prayer of thanks to God. The toast was hard and later on, I dislocated my jaw on one occasion on an exceptionally hard slice of bread while eating in too much of a hurry. (Perhaps it was a blessing in disguise as it made me a good listener and not much of a talker.) By a quarter past seven, the whole school had assembled in shorts and singlets for "drill" or what is nowadays called PE. This lasted half an hour. After a 15-minute break, we were ready for class at 8 am. Each lesson lasted 45 minutes and school ended at 1 pm. There was a recess of half an hour at 10.30 am for us to have a snack and a drink in the tiffin shed. 10 cents was enough for the noodles and *cendol* or sugared ice-water which were my favourite repast.

We were back in Horley Hall for lunch by a quarter past one as the hostel was a mere 300 yards from the main school building. Then followed a compulsory rest period of 45 minutes to an hour before we had to go downstairs to a classroom for the study hour (2.30 pm–4.30 pm). Homework had to be done and the next day's lessons prepared. A senior boy sat at a table in front like a teacher to ensure silence and discourage any chatting. He also made sure no one dozed off at his desk! Half past four was greeted with shouts of joy. We sprinted to the field to play on our own or sometimes take part in organised games like football or hockey. Athletics and even gymnastics could be practised but we had no swimming pool. The two hours of play were the best hours of the day. Dinner was at 7 pm after cold shower baths. Everyone had to be punctual. No excuses were accepted except in the case of illness. Punctuality became an ingrained habit all my life from my sojourn in Horley Hall. After dinner we were back in the study room reading or preparing for the next day. Half past nine was bedtime for all: lights out in all dormitories. Later when I became the prefect, it was my duty to ring the morning bell and to see to all the other chores of the day.

The discipline I learnt at Horley Hall was to be useful for the rest of my life for it developed regular habits of work and rest. Later on in Raffles College in Singapore and London University, I found it easy to rise early and buckle down to study. I believe well-run boarding schools for teenage children have an important role to play in developing disciplined habits even in cities like Singapore where distances from school are not so great.

We had no school on Saturday, so in the morning we were free to walk into town for a couple of hours to buy what we needed or luxuries like chocolates which some of us could afford. I had a monthly allowance of $5 which was a princely sum in the 1930s. It was certainly among the highest in Horley Hall as the majority of boarders were poor, and some were orphans supported by the Methodist Mission. The Methodists along with the Roman Catholics were great pioneers in fostering education in the Malay Peninsula and Singapore for boys and girls. Both countries owe a great debt of gratitude to these pioneers. The schools built in so many towns in the two countries stand as monuments to their enterprise and sense of religious mission. So many of us who emerged from their schools owe what we are and what we have achieved to their dedication, it was only more recently that the governments took over the main responsibility to educate their citizens but they have wisely left the missions to continue their good work.

Once a month we were allowed to see a film if and when Mr Kesselring thought there was a suitable one. As there was only one cinema in Ipoh at that time — the Sun Cinema, which I believe was the first venture of the famous Shaw Brothers who made a fortune out of the film business — our choice was limited. The cheapest price of a ticket was 10 cents (20 cents for adults) which entitled us to sit on hard wooden benches rather close to the screen. As I write this I wonder how Singapore schoolboys and girls today would react to being restricted to a single film a month or to be made to go to bed by 9.30 pm every night for that matter.

Talking of cinema-going reminds me of the time before I joined the boarding school when, accompanied by my friend Sunderaju, I went to see *Frankenstein*, a horror film. At one frightening moment, when the monster created by Frankenstein and acted by Boris Karloff, seemed to move menacingly towards the audience, I shut my eyes. When I opened them, my friend had vanished. He was hiding on the floor practically under the bench! On another occasion I went on my bicycle to see the original *Tarzan the Ape Man* which I enjoyed greatly. The way home at night to my bungalow in Jalan Bendahara lay past a Malay graveyard. Though I kept telling myself that there was little to fear, I found that I was cycling faster and faster with a palpitating heart, to arrive home panting, bathed in sweat. Never again did I venture alone to the cinema.

You may think that the restrictions imposed on us in Horley Hall were so severe that we were unhappy. On the contrary, I for one was really happy and never yearned to be out late at night except occasionally when there were boxing matches in Jubilee Park, an amusement centre that still exists today. I was enthralled by boxing and hero-worshipped the then world champion Joe Louis, the greatest fighter before Muhammad Ali. Apart from boxing there was little to tempt the boys to be out late. There were no all-night coffee-houses or discotheques, there were no garish cinema posters or seductive advertisements to titillate us. Our needs were simple and our energies were absorbed by football, hockey, basketball and athletics.

Sundays, however, were dull for most of us. The Sabbath was observed with Methodist strictness. We were not even supposed to whistle, let alone play games. But once the boarding master was out of sight we were on the field, especially when it rained. There was

Sunday School in the morning followed by a better-than-average lunch. In the evening we had to attend the service at the Wesley Church which still stands in the school compound today. Reading and studying occupied most of our Sundays until we grew old enough to appreciate the presence of girls in church. On the whole, Sunday was indeed a day of rest. Perhaps we were better able to face up to Mondays after our somnolent Sundays.

Chapter 5

Lessons

What did we learn in school? The curriculum was limited to the Arts, including Mathematics. We had a choice of English or Empire history and in ACS, we read about the kings and queens of England, their conquests and misdeeds. History began with the Battle of Bosworth Field in 1485 when Henry Tudor defeated the wicked Richard III who, according to Shakespeare cried out,

> A horse, a horse,
> My kingdom for a horse

when he was unhorsed and about to be slain. Our prescribed period ended in 1714 with the death of Queen Anne, the last of the Stuart dynasty. Queen Anne was not too bright so the famous satirical poet, Alexander Pope, in his *Rape of the Lock,* making fun of the trivial interests of English courtiers, says of her,

> And thou great Anna, whom three realms obey
> Dost sometimes counsel take, and sometimes tea
> (pronounced "tay")

The most interesting reign was that of Queen Elizabeth I, the "virgin queen" in the time of Shakespeare, the greatest poet and dramatist of all time, and such adventurers as Sir Walter Raleigh, a favourite of the Queen, who reputedly introduced tobacco and the potato into the British Isles from America and founded the colony of Virginia in America; Sir Francis Drake, the pirate who circumnavigated the globe and robbed several Spanish galleons of their treasure looted from the Incas and Aztecs of South America and Mexico. All this I found quite thrilling. I liked history as a subject and can tell you even the names of the six wives of Elizabeth's father, the corpulent Henry VIII, two of whom he executed when he got tired of them. One of his victims was Anne Boleyn, Elizabeth's mother, who is said to haunt the castle where she was imprisoned to this day! Henry VIII's reign is important historically for the separation of the Church of England from the Roman Catholic Church although ironically to this day, the English sovereign carries the title of the "Defender of the Faith" conferred by the Pope on Henry in his younger days. You will find "Fid. Def." on English coins to commemorate this.

Henry VIII, despite his cruelties, was an accomplished sports-man and poet in the days of his youth. In fact, many courtiers in the court of his daughter, Elizabeth, were men of many talents. The noble Sir Philip Sidney was a courtier, poet and soldier. He was wounded and dying in the battle of Zutphen in the Netherlands when he was offered a cup of water. Sir Philip gave the water to a wounded soldier who was lying beside him saying, "Thy need is greater than mine!" What a great and unselfish man! Another famous Elizabethan was Sir Walter Raleigh, a courtier, an adventurous sailor and a poet. When he fell out of favour with Elizabeth's successor, the King of England James I who ordered his execution, Raleigh left the following poem in his Bible the night before his death:

> Even such is Time, that takes in trust
> Our youth, our joys, our all we have,
> And pays us but with earth and dust;
> Who in the dark and silent grave,
> When we have wander'd all our ways,
> Shuts up the story of our days;
> But from this earth, this grave, this dust,
> My God will raise me up, I trust.

I was also interested in the rebellion led by Oliver Cromwell and his well-trained model army of "Ironsides" or "Roundheads" (close-cropped heads) against the "Cavaliers" of King Charles I whose long shoulder-length hair later became fashionable in the West, especially among rock bands.

The civil war was a struggle between the King and Parliament as to who should rule England. King Charles I believed in the "divine right of kings" to rule and levy taxes whereas Parliament, which consisted of the people's representatives, defied the King and insisted on its own supremacy. Parliament, led by Oliver Cromwell, eventually won after many battles. Cromwell was a Puritan and a very religious dictator who had King Charles I executed one January morning in 1649. The King went bravely to his death and his courage was celebrated by the poet Andrew Marvell, a supporter of Cromwell.

> He nothing common did or mean
> Upon that memorable Scene
> But with his keener Eye
> The Axes edge did try
> Nor call'd the Gods with vulgar spight

To vindicate his helpless Right
But bow'd his comely Head
Down as upon a Bed

Cromwell was a great soldier who never lost a battle. He crushed the Irish and the Scots in separate battles. A couple of anecdotes about Cromwell bear telling. While crossing a river in Ireland he told his troops, "Put your trust in God but keep your powder (gunpowder) dry." Religious but practical too! On another occasion when he invaded Scotland, the Scots under General Leslie held a superior tactical position on hilly ground. Leslie's Presbyterian followers, feeling sure that God was on their side, urged him to attack Cromwell's army. Leslie reluctantly did this and as his forces surged forward, Cromwell realised that his opponent had made a mistake. He exclaimed, "The Lord has delivered them into our hands" and proceeded to inflict a disastrous defeat on the Scots!

Cromwell's dictatorship from 1649 to 1658 was unpopular as he closed theatres and all places of entertainment which he considered sinful. England was admired abroad for her strength under Cromwell but the English on the whole were glad when he died. They lost little time in inviting the son of Charles I to return from France where he had taken refuge. The restoration of the monarchy in 1660 was widely welcomed and to this day, England has retained the rule of kings and queens even though most countries have got rid of them and established republics. Charles II was an amiable, pleasure-loving ruler who wisely avoided punishing those who had dethroned his father. All he did was to order the corpses of his worst enemies like Cromwell and a couple of followers to be dug up and hung! Macabre but merciful! The great poet John Milton who was an enthusiastic supporter of Cromwell was spared. Milton, who was blind by this time, dictated his great epic poem *Paradise Lost* to his three daughters. All university students of English Literature have to study this epic poem. No doubt some of them may wish at times that Charles II had disposed of John Milton before he wrote *Paradise Lost!*

We did learn something of European movements like the Renaissance and the Reformation led by the German monk Martin Luther, but our main interest was English history.

Much as I liked history I loved literature more. My interest in this subject was stimulated by a series of school textbooks called *Highroads of Literature* which were lavishly illustrated in colour. My imagination caught fire at the tales of the gallant knights of King Arthur's Round Table, especially the heroic Sir Lancelot and the saintly Sir Galahad, who sought the Holy Grail and whose "strength was as the strength of ten because his heart was pure". Then there were the adventures of Sir Gawain and the Green Knight, who insisted that Sir Gawain should chop off his head provided in a year's time Sir Gawain returned to let him chop off Sir Gawain's head! The Green Knight, who had magical powers, just picked up his own severed head, mounted his horse and rode off! Would Sir Gawain keep his word and return at the end of the year to certain death? What do you think? As a matter of fact, he did, as noble knights always kept their promises. What do you suppose happened when Sir Gawain heard the Green Knight sharpening his sword as he approached the site where they first met? The Green Knight went through all the motions of cutting off Sir Gawain's head but spared him in the end for his indomitable courage in keeping his promise. He merely nicked Sir Gawain's neck with his sword.

The heroic and the romantic are the stuff to stir the minds and hold the interest of the young. In my day we had no Superman, Spiderman, Ultraman or the Ninja Turtles to fight and triumph over evil. But we had tales of heroes like Beowulf of the old English epic who fought the evil man-eating monster Grendal in the depths of a lake; we had tales of Robin Hood and his merry men of Sherwood

Forest who robbed the rich to give to the poor and foil the plots of the evil Sheriff of Nottingham. Robin Hood has, of course, been the subject of many films through the years. In school we read the historical novels of Sir Walter Scott like *Ivanhoe* and *Kenilworth* replete with plots and rescues, knightly tournaments on horseback and beautiful ladies. One of the set texts for what was then known as the Junior Cambridge class (equivalent to the year before "O" levels nowadays; the examination was set and marked in England) was the poem *Hiawatha* by the American poet Henry Wadsworth Longfellow, which presented the Red Indians as loving and suffering people and not the tomahawk-wielding savages out to scalp white men as depicted in cowboy films. *Hiawatha,* which appealed to us, was enjoyed by the whole class.

We studied two plays of Shakespeare, *Julius Caesar* in the Junior Cambridge and the romantic comedy *As You Like It* in our Senior class. These delighted me and so began a lifelong love for Shakespeare. His profound understanding of human beings as shown in his comedies and tragedies has, I believe, never been equalled in all literature. Even as schoolboys we could appreciate Shakespeare's portrayal of the idealistic Brutus, the practical but envious Cassius and the cunning oratory of Mark Antony who is able to turn the mob against the conspirators in *Julius Caesar.* It is in his tragedies like *Hamlet, Othello, Macbeth* and *King Lear* that Shakespeare explores and reveals men's minds and motives in his superb blank verse. I have perhaps learnt more about human nature from Shakespeare than from reading modern psychologists.

Literature should only be taught by teachers who are enthusiastic and who love the subject. This love inspires the pupils. The Ipoh Anglo-Chinese School was blessed with such teachers, none of whom were university graduates except for the Americans. The local staff were called "normal-trained" teachers who had undergone three years' training in teaching methods. They were keen and dedicated. Students can always sense whether a teacher is really interested in his subject. We were lucky to have such good teachers in our school in the 1930s. They earned little — none ever owned a car as far as I know — but they taught well. Nowhere in the world are teachers paid as well as they should be, so no one who yearns after wealth should become a teacher.

Next to Literature I was fond of Religious Knowledge as found in our set texts, the *Gospel according to Luke* and the Acts *of the Apostles* in the King James' 1611 version. The best scholars of the day co-operated to produce this version of the Bible so the language is of surpassing beauty. I was much moved by the rhythm of the prose and even more by the life of Jesus as narrated by St Luke. Passages describing the agony in the garden of Gethsamane and Christ weeping over Jerusalem moved me to tears. It was easy for me to excel in this subject as in Literature as I read and reread the texts for the sheer music of the words. It was the love for the language of literature, both poetry and prose, that made me reject the advice of my teachers (and later of friends) that I should study law. They did this because I was the school's leading debater. I would probably have become rich like my lawyer friends, some of whom even own racehorses, but I preferred to become a teacher. Teaching can be such a rewarding and satisfying job if teachers are not overloaded with administrative tasks.

Chapter 6

School Activities

W hen I was in the School Certificate Class in 1936, our new progressive American principal, Percy B Bell, made us sit for an intelligence and aptitude test to help us choose our future careers. This test was based on some American educational research and we were graded according to the points we scored. We were also required to fill in a questionnaire listing the sort of jobs we wanted to do upon leaving school. In those days, nearly all school-leavers went to work after passing the Cambridge School Certificate examinations as very few aspired to pursue higher studies either at Raffles College or at the Medical College in Singapore. One of my classmates who was more daring and mischievous than the rest of us listed his ambition to be a dance hall manager or a horse-racing tipster! This was a great shock to the teachers and the students as the Methodist mission consistently frowned on any form of gambling, alcohol or dancing (except folk dancing). At least one teacher who frequented the cabaret in Jubilee Park and patronised the taxi dancers found himself transferred to the backwoods of Telok Anson where there was no dance hall. Most of us expected that our classmate would be expelled. The principal, more liberal than his predecessors, was content to let him off with a warning. The interesting thing about this story is that my classmate did eventually become a well-known racing expert in Malaya and Singapore under the pseudonym of Epsom Jeep. He had been serious in his intentions while we assumed he was merely being cheeky!

Our time in school galloped swiftly by as time always does when you are young, active and happy. But you hardly notice it whereas as you grow older, you become more conscious of the passing years. Every alternate year, our school put on a Shakespeare play or a concert by the school orchestra for charity. I recall the first stage play I ever saw was when I was in one of the lower forms. The teachers and the senior pupils performed Shakespeare's best comedy *Twelfth Night* or *What You Will* for three nights. A special matinee performance was put on for the benefit of the younger pupils. The mission schools were culturally active and the pupils had time enough to take part in plays and concerts.

It was a matter of indifference to us that we were members of the far-flung British Empire on which the sun never set. One school-day every year was set aside as "Empire Day" — the whole school assembled for a reading of the Empire Day Message (a duty I was called upon to perform more than once) after which school was dismissed. King George V's Silver Jubilee was celebrated in 1935 on the town *padang* where all the schoolchildren in Ipoh were assembled in the hot sun. By this time schoolboys were no longer compelled to wear cork helmets to prevent sunstroke. (The British at first underestimated the inbuilt attribute of Asians to withstand the heat of the sun but later allowed us to go bareheaded. The manufacturers of cork helmets went bankrupt as a consequence.) All I remember of Empire Day celebrations is that we were each given an Eskimo Pie ice-cream which we enjoyed with relish in the heat of the sun. We were not aware of the propaganda reason for the celebration. It was all too subtle for our immature minds. Some of us were rather happy in our History lessons to learn that God intervened on behalf of England in 1588 to disperse and sink the great Spanish Armada of heavily armed galleons by stirring up a storm. It was many years later and in totally different circumstances during the Japanese Occupation when I was told that God had also intervened with a "divine wind" (*kamikaze*) to destroy Kublai Khan's fleet on behalf of Japan that I became sceptical. As I was then an unwilling denizen of Japan's Greater East Asia Co-prosperity Sphere where all suffered and nobody prospered, I deemed it an error on the part of the heavenly powers not to have allowed Kublai Khan to do unto the samurai of Japan what the Japanese soldiers did to us!

Although our History lessons were almost wholly British orientated, Geography was mainly Asian. We learnt a great deal about the mountains, rivers and plains of India and China as well as the monsoon lands of South-East Asia. We drew endless maps of the Malay Peninsula paying special attention to our State of Perak, famous for its production of tin. Our teachers arranged visits to tin mines and other interesting places, including a coffee plantation and the Kledang and Maxwell hill stations.

The most exciting geographical tour was arranged during the school vacation in 1934. Our enterprising Geography master had planned to take us by bus in a leisurely fashion to the Colony of Singapore via Malacca where we stayed a day and night admiring the historical relics of the Portuguese and Dutch conquests. We were put up in a school building for the night. We spent another night in Segamat in Johor where we had to book into a cheap third-rate lodging house as our hosts had failed to arrange any accommodation for us. Difficulties did not bother us youngsters who were thrilled at the prospect of seeing Singapore — a great port none of us had ever visited before and of which we had heard so much. Singapore was the ultimate in city life in the imagination of schoolchildren in Malaya. I, for one, had heard of the famous dome of the Capitol Cinema which appeared to be an architectural wonder! I am sure Singaporeans growing up now amidst the city's cloud-capped towers and its massive shopping centres would laugh at the idea of naive upcountry children gazing at the Capitol dome as a monumental masterpiece! But in the 1930s, there was little in Malaya to match it or to compare with it and the magnificent St Andrew's Cathedral for instance. We were also deeply impressed by Raffles Hotel which we were not allowed to enter. It was a white man's preserve. In any case, none of us could have afforded to cross its portals. Fortunately, these early monuments of Singapore have been preserved for posterity although many others have given way to modern developments.

We schoolboys stayed in Oldham Hall which was the boarding school for those studying in ACS, Singapore. Oldham Hall was

A visit to the limestone caves in Ipoh. Notice the cork helmets and felt hats worn by all the boys.

situated in Barker Road, behind the school building which still stands. We went on a sightseeing tour visiting the Botanic Gardens and Alkaff Gardens (now no more a garden but Sennet Estate). We visited the Jade House (now gone too), the property of the Tiger Balm King Aw Boon Haw and saw its wonderful collections. I do not remember much else of what I saw of Singapore in the 1934 visit but I was destined to live in the city from 1938 to 1941 when I joined Raffles College in Bukit Timah Road.

The impact made on us by our keen Geography master showed up eventually in the Cambridge School Certificate examinations in 1936 when my class scored eight distinctions in the subject out of a class of about 30. I have already mentioned the quality of our teachers. Perhaps it was not so much what they taught but the way they taught us. I remember some of them with respect and affection. They cared for each of us as individuals. One of our teachers went to Britain after the war, in 1948, to read Law when I was myself an undergraduate in London University. He returned to Ipoh a barrister but died within two years in his early fifties. *Sic vita.*

I completed my School Certificate examinations in 1936 and could have joined Raffles College as I scored distinctions in every subject except Mathematics in which I had a credit pass. Raffles College merely required credits in English, Mathematics and two other subjects for admission into the Arts course. We had no science classes in ACS, Ipoh. An extension to the school building was planned to accommodate a laboratory for science teaching only in 1937. I don't think any school in Ipoh was equipped to teach Science in my time. Singapore and Penang were more advanced in this respect.

My teachers persuaded me to stay another year in school as the ACS decided to begin a Matriculation class for the first time in 1937. In any case, I was keen to extend my happy school-days. My father had no objection, so I stayed another year in Ipoh. The class was a

The first ACS Matriculation class (1937). Maurice Baker is standing in the centre; Toh Chin Chye is seated on the extreme left.

Maurice Baker's younger brother Leonard, who died in his twenties.

mixed one which included three girls among its numbers. Among those who joined us from other Perak schools was Toh Chin Chye, who was destined to become an eminent politician and eventually the Deputy Prime Minister of Singapore. There were others who became famous doctors and lawyers in Malaya and Singapore after the Japanese Occupation. I believe ACS, Ipoh, pioneered the Matriculation class. We had to go to Singapore for the Matriculation examination set by London University. Victoria School in Jalan Besar was the examination centre. Strangely enough, 15 years later I was to teach in this same school for nearly two years.

The one sadness of my otherwise happy childhood and adolescence was my younger brother's epilepsy. He suffered his first attack at the age of nine when he was in Horley Hall with me. I thought at first that he had merely fainted but the subsequent fits were frightening to see. The doctor could only administer sedatives. There was no cure. Nowadays there are drugs to reduce the number and violence of the attacks but not in the 1930s and 1940s. The poor boy suffered greatly, puzzled by his ailment, and we suffered with him, especially during the Japanese Occupation when no drugs were available. We couldn't help him. We could only watch over him, making sure he did not injure himself in his sudden falls when a fit seized him. All of us were alert and tense all the time, watching out for his violent seizures. He died in his twenties and I think he preferred to go rather than suffer so much.

Chapter 7

Raffles College 1938–1941

M alaya under the British was divided into the Federated Malay States and the Unfederated Malay States which were ruled by the Sultans with British resident advisers. Power really rested with the advisers except in matters of religion and traditional customs. Penang, Singapore and Malacca constituted the Straits Settlements which were colonies directly administered by the Colonial Office in London. Tertiary education was available only in Singapore in Raffles College which was officially opened in 1929 mainly for the training of teachers, and the King Edward VII Medical College which had been established in 1905. Admission to this institution was the same as for Raffles College. I could have joined the Medical College if I had wanted to. First year medical students had to come to Raffles College for courses in Physics and Chemistry. Nowadays admission to read for a medical degree is so fiercely competitive that some who could have become doctors without difficulty are denied admission. Yet the doctors who graduated in the earlier years were of the highest quality and many distinguished themselves in the service of their fellowmen.

Generally speaking, the doctors before the war received an all-round education and were perhaps better read as they were not made to join the Science stream early in secondary school as is done nowadays. I have some doubts about the effects of too early specialisation on the minds and personalities of students. But this is a controversial subject. I was fortunate to follow my own inclinations in what I wanted to study. I was not subjected to any parental pressure to be a doctor or a lawyer. I wanted to be a teacher, inspired as I was by my own teachers who thought, however, that I should read law. I could have applied for a scholarship to Raffles College as there were ten open to Singapore and Malaya but my father thought I should not deprive some deserving poor boy or girl who needed the scholarship. He said that he could support me without any difficulty. A Raffles College scholarship was worth $720 a year. It was enough to pay tuition fees, the hostel charges, to buy clothes and to have something left over for pocket money. Clothes were formal. All students had to wear a tie and appear in a full suit of white drill at every lecture. We also had to dress for dinner! Remember that there was no air-conditioning then, only fans. On one occasion at a History lecture by Professor Dyer, who always entered the class in full regalia in his gown and mortar board, he noticed that one of the students had taken off his jacket. I recall vividly Professor Dyer's order, "You! Remove your naked presence from my immediate vicinity!"

I entered Raffles College as a private student but won an exhibition of $500 without having to apply for it based on the results of the first year examinations. At the end of my second year, I was awarded a full scholarship as I headed the examination lists. I felt really rich as my father had continued to pay my fees. I could treat my friends to the cinema, to lunches, and even pay bus and taxi fares. I have never had so many friends as I had in Raffles College!

I enjoyed their company even if I had to pay a little for the pleasure and I still feel nostalgic about them despite their taking ways.

Ragging

The thought of joining Raffles College had its terrors. We heard rumours that freshmen were subjected to brutal ragging but no details were known. Vague imaginings are worse than known fears and my imagination worked overtime exaggerating the unknown. The train from Ipoh to Singapore on which I travelled stayed four hours at the Kuala Lumpur station before leaving at 10 pm to arrive in Singapore early in the morning at 7 am. I scanned the KL platform anxiously for menacing "seniors" but the only one I spotted as a likely bully was an Indian lad with a swanky scarf slung around his neck and a brown felt hat perched at a jaunty angle on his head. He exuded supreme confidence in his blue blazer and razor-sharp pants. It was only the next morning, after crossing the causeway and sharing a taxi from the station to the college, that I discovered he was a fellow freshman or "freshie" as we were called by the senior students. Staggering with our bags from the taxi to the portals of the Eu Tong Sen block, we were deluged by buckets of water from the balcony above. My companion, who was one day destined to be a High Court judge in Malaysia, was as soaked as I was. The shared humiliation made us fast friends for years to come. We had to suffer more than humiliation from a few sadistic senior students though most of them limited themselves to good-humoured witty verbal darts and paper bullets of the brain. We were forced to wear a truncated green tie of coarse texture throughout the first term and humbly addressed our seniors as "sir" whenever we met them. We avoided them as much as possible though this was difficult for the hostelites but much easier for the day students from Singapore. When the ragging went beyond bearable limits, my friend, Fred, and I organised a revolt, but we were betrayed. We were subjected to a "kangaroo" court trial and sentenced to extra ducking in a large porcelain tub. My head was forcibly held back below the tap while the water was directed in a jet against my nostrils. The normal ducking was when one was lifted by two or three seniors, feet well above the head which was pushed under water for ten or so seconds repeatedly. The college authorities got wind of the fact that the ragging was getting out of control. Two of the senior students were suspended from Raffles College for a term. Ragging is a controversial issue but I myself have no doubt that it is indefensible and a wholly unnecessary introduction to higher education. Years later when I attended King's College in London University, the senior students welcomed us and invited us to join various college societies and helped us to find our way around.

At times mass ragging could be amusing, as when the freshmen were assembled at dawn in the upper quadrangle of Raffles College and marched down to the field for morning exercises. I was chosen to carry a flag and lead the group as I was tall. The shortest boy was bestowed the title of "bad egg". We were placed under the command of the senior "bad egg". The exercises we had to undergo were strenuous but most of us were fit enough to take the ragging well. One evening we were all assembled and marched off to the Botanic Gardens which used to be open to the public at night. The seniors had spread a rumour that a graduate with a fearsome reputation as a ragger was coming especially to deal with us. He was a torture master, we were warned. Such rumours demoralised us as they were meant to. While we waited in trepidation, a tall, slim and rather mild-looking Chinese arrived who did not seem to fit the role of a demon ragger. We received our marching orders and trudged off in ragged ranks to the centre of the gardens where there was a

Maurice Baker (extreme right) with other Raffles Collegians in his room in 1939.

Raffles College in 1938

bandstand. Each freshmen was ordered to entertain the seniors by singing a song under a clear October moon.

We freshmen fell into line and waited till a commanding senior voice ordered, "Freshie advance and sing. You better be good or else!"

A nervous freshman stepped forward and attempted a "pop" song. He didn't get far.

"Stop! Stop!" roared a senior voice. "You call that singing? Run around the bandstand three times! Pretender!"

The next freshman was dismissed too, the next and the next in swift order. It was apparent that the seniors were amusing themselves by humiliating us. It didn't matter in the least whether one's voice was raucous or mellifluous, whether one sang in tune or croaked out of tune, the reaction of the critical audience was the same. Everyone of us was booed at and made to run three times round the bandstand while acid comments were made on our attempts to sing. This was quite funny so we took it in good spirit.

We were then marched off to the pond in the Botanic Gardens and ordered to line up in a single row on its edge. The "seniors" loudly discussed the depth of the pond and the unfortunate drowning the previous year. "Surrender your wallets and other valuables," ordered a senior. "Those who cannot swim put up your hands," yelled the leader. Mine was one of many hands that shot up! "We want to encourage co-operation among the freshies," said the senior-in-charge. "Therefore those who can swim are to save the non-swimmers. It won't be our fault if you let anyone drown." We were really scared that we were about to be pushed into the pond. We waited in suspense for a minute or two but nothing happened. Outbursts of senior laughter made us realise that the joke was on us! We were then dismissed to find our way back out of the gardens. A kind second-year undergraduate, who claimed to know his way like the back of his hand, led us singing all the way until all of a sudden with a strangulated cry, he disappeared into a hidden pool. We had to rescue the soaked senior whose singing ceased. But he did show us the rest of the way home. I must say that I enjoyed the whole episode and chuckled over it many a time over the years.

The hostel warden whose job it was to maintain discipline invariably made himself scarce when the seniors were on their ragging rampage. He pretended not to know what was happening. Mr Edwards was a kindly old gentleman who was himself some-times the victim of undergraduate pranks. The poor man's flat was situated in the middle with 20 student cubicles to the left of him and 20 cubicles to the right of him. A long corridor linked the two. "Down this corridor tin cans clattered and clanged past his door in the wee hours of the night. He would rush down the corridors threatening, "I'll touch your pockets, I'll touch your pockets", meaning that he would fine us. He never did for he never caught anyone. Once a prankster set off firecrackers outside his door! He had a dilapidated old junk of a car which also suffered untold indignities.

The Eu Tong Sen building which housed us eventually became part of the University of Singapore's departments of English, History, Malay and Chinese Studies. Today it is part of the National Institute of Education's Bukit Timah campus. The very cubicles where we lived were converted into offices and I was destined to tutor students in English Literature in the 1960s and 70s in the very rooms where I had lived in the 1930s.

The more scholarly and serious senior undergraduates took no part in the ragging. One of these, Goh Keng Swee, was already recognised as a brilliant economist who was invited by Professor Silcock, Head of the Economics Department, to tutor the first year students. Lim Kim San was frequently spotted in Goh's company. We never approached or spoke to them, merely admiring them from a distance. Among the senior students was also the late Hon Sui Sen from Penang, as refined, kindly and considerate as ever. All three were destined to become distinguished ministers in the Singapore cabinet later in life.

Among the freshmen of the 1938 to 1939 intake were several from the Malay States who eventually became top civil servants in independent Malaysia. These included Syed Zahirrudin who was appointed High Commissioner to the United Kingdom and later Governor of Malacca, and Singapore scholar Kwan Sai Kheong who made his mark as Director of Education and later as Vice-chancellor of the National University of Singapore. He was my best friend. He succeeded me as Ambassador to the Republic of the Philippines and sadly died in Manila of throat cancer in 1981 at the age of 61. It was the 1940 to 1941 intake which produced two Prime Ministers in Abdul Razak of Malaysia and Lee Kuan Yew of Singapore. Tun Razak passed away in 1976 and Mr Lee handed over the reins of power to Mr Goh Chok Tong in November 1990.

Chapter 8

Raffles College Teaching Staff

What was our daily routine in Raffles College like? We had lectures about five or six times a week, each lecture lasting about 50 minutes or so. We had to hand in an essay every week and attend tutorials in the three subjects of our choice. A tutorial meant two students at a time facing the lecturer for an hour, answering probing questions on our essays. We had to convince the lecturer or professor that we really understood the subject and knew what we had written about. The tutorial is the most important part of university training as it develops critical thinking and accurate, succinct writing. The tutorial is essential for all arts subjects. In Raffles College we had only English Literature, History, Geography, Economics and Mathematics. The Science students in my time had to do laboratory experiments in Chemistry and Physics in the afternoons while the Arts undergraduates spent their time reading in the library. There was always a great deal of reading to be done.

We students in Raffles College got to know each other well as there were only about a hundred of us in the hostel in both Arts and

Science in the first, second and final years. We knew our lecturers and professors personally too. The most interesting character among the staff was the Professor of History, W E Dyer, who was never without his cap and academic gown at lectures. He had a good sense of humour but occasionally cut a caustic comment as, for example, when he told an Indian undergraduate who had scored less than 30 marks in history, "Young man, I advise you not to throw your father's money in the drain any longer. Leave the college and learn to drive a bullock cart for a living!" Once when a number of boys were waiting outside Dyer's office to collect their essays and were chatting away noisily, he suddenly emerged and thundered, "Would you mind not behaving like a wounded herd of buffaloes?" Stunned silence. He then turned on his heels and strode serenely back into his office.

He was in the middle of a lecture once in Oei Tiong Ham Hall (now demolished) when he looked up at the gallery where our library was housed and noticed the trousered leg of a male student hanging through the railings. He said loudly, "Would you mind moving that leg of mutton out of my sight?" The unfortunate victim was nicknamed "leg of mutton" for the rest of his career in college. I remember another incident when Professor Dyer found that one of the fans in the lecture hall had not been switched on. He said, "Would one of you mind setting that mechanical device rotating upon its axis?" A sly half-smile.

Despite his rather pompous style and somewhat formal manner, Professor Dyer was a middle-aged bachelor with a kind heart as I was to discover during the war. But before that, he once called me into his office and advised me to tell my sister, who was in her first year, not to sit right in the front row in his class correcting my lecture notes. Professor Dyer gave the same lectures year after year, like most university staff in certain subjects. I had given my sister my lecture notes which she coolly took into the lecture hall and just followed the lecture, concentrating on my notes instead of pretending to take down the words of the professor. This upset the good professor so he admonished me! I suppose it was because I gave her my lecture notes. I gave my sister a good scolding for getting me into trouble!

When the Japanese attacked Malaya and bombed Singapore, I was a volunteer member of the Raffles College Medical Auxiliary Service which had been hastily organised to pick up casualties of the bombing as well as to perform other duties. It was my turn to do some roof-spotting one day, that is, looking out for enemy planes. It so happened that morning, I looked up at the sky, a Cold Storage pork pie in one hand, I suddenly saw the leading planes of a Japanese squadron through a break in the clouds. Immediately I pressed the alarm bell though the sirens had not sounded and in fact did not go off till 30 or 40 seconds later. So Professor Dyer trudged up to my watching post during the raid and commented, "A keen bit of spotting that!" He then proceeded to chat with me about my future as I had then been awarded the prestigious Queen's Scholarship after my final examinations in 1941. In pre-war days, this scholarship meant admission to Oxford or Cambridge. Throughout our conversation he remained calm, oblivious to the bombing raid while I listened nervously in our exposed position. Normally we had to take shelter during a raid in the buildings below. Professor Dyer was kindness itself.

All our teachers were from the United Kingdom, though the very best of our own graduates became tutors or demonstrators in Science. It was not till well after the war that Malayans and Singaporeans became lecturers. The two English lecturers whom I got to know best were Professor L F Casson and Graham Hough who assisted him. Both were to become eminent authorities in their special fields of study after the war. Professor Casson was fortunate enough to leave before the Japanese captured Singapore, but Graham

Hough suffered three and a half years of internment like Professor Dyer and several other members of the Raffles College teaching staff. Some died in internment.

Professor Casson was a frail, slightly hunched, chain-smoking scholar whose special interest was Anglo-Saxon and Middle English. Graham Hough taught Shakespeare and more modern literature including the Romantic poets like Wordsworth, Keats and Shelley. They were the only two members of the English Department staff who had to deal with the wide range of English Literature. We enjoyed some breezy and informative lectures. Both of them mixed well with their students and were never aloof unlike British colonial officials. It was in Professor Casson's house that I had my first taste of beer — a bitter brew that I did not like at first though I did get used to it years later in the UK. Professor Casson invited three of us — perhaps he considered us his best students — to a free holiday in Cameron Highlands for a week. Graham Hough who was in his twenties and hence only a few years older than us, used to travel second-class on the Federated Malay States railway to be in our company. He was probably the only Englishman not travelling first-class. He did not bother to maintain the status of a member of the ruling race. Both our teachers seemed oblivious of race barriers so we were relaxed in their company. Years later when I went to England, Professor Casson was instrumental in getting me admitted to King's College, London University. I was fortunate to be his student once again. He left in the 1960s to teach in South Africa where he is reported to have died in 1967. Mr Hough has attained fame in Cambridge with several learned publications. He passed away in 1990.

Among the other lecturers, I remember the late Mr Amon who taught Geography from notes yellowed with age. Geography was then mostly concerned with physical, human and regional aspects of the world. It was more an arts than a science subject but no doubt it has become more scientific nowadays. Academic studies have their fashions like women's clothes and many arts subjects aspired to be scientific when science became the rage in academia. But to get back to Mr Amon. He was a chain-smoker whose fingers were nicotine-yellow like his notes. He could be seen puffing away before a lecture, and as no smoking was allowed during lectures, he was out of the classroom in 40 minutes. When we emerged we would see him lighting up a cigarette with shaky hands!

Chapter 9

College Life

College student life in the 1930s was peaceful and tame compared to the 1960s when university students in Europe, the United States and elsewhere including Malaysia and Singapore were fighting for academic freedom. The 1960s were years of academic turmoil and some institutions of higher learning had to be closed temporarily. Things are much quieter now, perhaps even as they were in the 1930s. We had no political interests, being content with pursuing our studies while the colonial government maintained law and order.

A hundred of us who stayed in the hostel had to obey strict rules — breakfast had to be eaten in the dining hall before 7.30 am, lunch between 12 noon and 2 pm, and dinner sharp at 7.30 pm. Dress for breakfast was optional but latecomers forfeited their meals. Silence had to be observed throughout the hostel from 2 pm to 4.30 pm after which nearly everyone ran out to the playing fields for sports activities while the musicians scraped their violins in their rooms as much as they pleased. One of our violinists was the late Kwan Sai Kheong who was a talented musician as well as an artist.

He wasted no time. At 4.30 pm sharp, we would hear him strike the first musical notes on his favourite instrument. As I was more interested in sports than music, I was among the first on the field or the tennis courts.

Raffles College in the 1930s fielded some of the best teams in Singapore in a number of games like hockey, rugger, football and cricket as the old records will bear testimony. Some of our star players were chosen for the state team. I am told that most undergraduates nowadays are too absorbed in their studies to bother about games.

After dinner we had to study, so silence was observed. All room lights were switched off by 11 pm but the staircases remained well-lit all night. Examination time meant that the staircases were in full use. Large numbers of students clustered like moths under the light with books and notes.

Hostelites were permitted to stay out till 11 pm twice a month on Saturdays. We had to obtain permission and sign the late-night book before going out. Anyone caught returning later than 11 pm paid a fine of $2. Noisemakers and impromptu bathroom baritones were also subjected to instant justice ($2) if caught. All in all, I am sure we were more carefully guarded than girl hostelites nowadays.

Nights out were big occasions. It was Saturday night fever all right. The way into town was by taxi (yellow top or check cabs belonging to the Cycle and Carriage Co) which cost 40 cents from the Bukit Timah campus to the Capitol Theatre. Four could share the taxi. The alternative was to walk across the field (now part of the Botanic Gardens) to Bukit Timah Road and catch a "mosquito" bus which carried fewer than ten passengers to Queen Street at 10 cents each. Once at the bus terminus, we used the Singapore Traction Company electric trams which ran on rails using overhead wires. These were noisy vehicles that rattled along clang-clanging loudly to get rickshaws and pedestrians out of the way. One could also

Maurice Baker in his twenties.

ride a rickshaw but I for one felt a little uneasy about the poor man sweating between the shafts running along on the road.

There were two large cinemas, the old Alhambra on Beach Road and the Capitol which still survives today, and a smaller one, the Pavilion which was on Orchard Road where the Specialist Centre now stands. The Cathay opened later, just months before the Japanese onslaught. If my mental album is right, the first picture shown at the Cathay was *The Four Feathers*. There were three large amusement parks — the Great World in Kim Seng Road, the Happy World (later renamed the Gay World) in Geylang and the New World in Jalan Besar. As the Great World was nearest to Raffles College, it was the one most popular among us. There were numerous shooting galleries, open gambling stalls with tins of cigarettes as prizes, a Chinese opera house and a Malay *bangsawan* theatre. Malay and Chinese culture were very much alive then, needing no government promotion or subsidies. There was a boxing ring where imported boxers, especially from the Philippines and Thailand, exhibited their skills. There was also a cabaret with taxi dancers which cost one 25 cents for a three-minute dance to music provided by a live dance band. The dances were the ballroom type — the waltz, foxtrot, quickstep and rumba, etc. The wild rock-and-roll had not been created yet though there was a popular group dance called the Lambeth Walk. A few undergraduates became keen and expert dancers. The traditional Malay *ronggeng* was staged in the open air on an elevated platform to the accompaniment of a violin and drums. Some of the Malay undergrads tried to teach me how to move to this rather graceful dance where one never touches one's partner.

One main shopping centre, especially for writing materials, was in Change Alley, off Collyer Quay. This was a narrow lane crowded with shops of every description where everything was available and could be bargained for. But Middle Road was the best place for shoes — handmade-to-measure shoes. A pair of such elegant fitting shoes cost less than $5. Tailors were to be found all along North Bridge Road to sew the white drill cotton suits, the standard outfit in college. Later "sharkskin" suits became popular, but they were expensive. High Street and Raffles Place were the fashionable shopping centres in Singapore, not Orchard Road. Robinsons, John Little's, Whiteaways (now no more), all in Raffles Place, were the classy department stores of the 1930s but we rarely stepped into these luxury stores because of their relatively high prices. No bargaining was permitted in these places.

Bookshops were few indeed, but all along Bras Basah Road there were veritable treasure houses of second-hand books in a row of small shops (now demolished). Educational books were cheap and plentiful. The National Library was in the present Raffles Museum but Raffles College had its own small library of course. Many of the books were destroyed by Japanese troops when they overran the Bukit Timah Campus which became the Headquarters of the Japanese armed forces during the occupation. The MPH bookshop existed at its iconic site at the junction of Stamford Road and Hill Street but in a smaller building if my memory serves me right. Another well-known bookshop was the Kelly and Walsh establishment. There were a few Chinese bookshops which also sold stationery.

The most exciting events of our lives in Raffles College were the annual matches we played against the King Edward VII Medical College in football, rugger, hockey, cricket and the inter-college athletics meet. Tension built up before each contest and the day itself had something of a battle atmosphere. There was nothing friendly about any of the games. The barracking was loud and often rude, though sometimes witty and amusing. One medical student who was a good cricketer but who had failed his exams more than once was subjected to insults in order to demoralise him. Outsiders might have thought that the supporters of the teams would come to blows but this never happened during the years I was in college. I was told though that in 1935 or 1936, there had been a free-for-all on the rugger field during which hired wooden chairs had been smashed.

Raffles College often won the contests as we had excellent sportsmen like E W Barker who eventually became Singapore's Minister of Law when she achieved independence. I recall one occasion when the late Tun Abdul Razak, Prime Minister of Malaysia from 1970 to 1976, played as a wing forward in our soccer team. He was speedy and at a crucial moment, when the scores were tied a couple of minutes before the end, he made a great run down the wing and shot the ball from a difficult angle. The medical goalkeeper rushed out but the ball swerved past him and the rest of the defenders into the goal. We won and Razak was the hero of the day. Years later in 1970 when I was Singapore's High Commissioner to Malaysia, I teased him at a party, claiming that a lucky freak breeze had blown the ball into the goal. He laughingly maintained that it was a special Pélé "banana kick" of his which had won the day. Memories of our days in Raffles College led to close friendships which proved useful even in difficult times when Malaysia and Singapore had many differences and faced some problems.

Victory at an inter-college game was boisterously celebrated. We carried the challenge trophy round to the homes of lecturers and professors who generously filled the large silver cups with cold beer. On those rare occasions when the medicos won, they used to drive round our campus in chartered buses screaming their heads off. Once we prepared a cold wet reception for them by turning water hoses on them to cool their exuberance!

Apart from the inter-college games, there was the annual seniors-versus-freshmen series which was just about the nearest thing to murder! The freshmen, who had never played together as a team, were confronted by the college first team. There could only be one result in such a contest. It was as if our Geylang soccer team was up against Manchester United, the 1993 English champions. The result would be nothing short of a football massacre. The freshmen were trounced, especially in rugger. If ever there was a chance of an upset as in hockey or soccer, the referee, who was always a senior, would award a penalty or two against the freshmen to settle the issue. In my first year we had some excellent players like our rugger stand-off, Cheong Weng Choong and Sheik Hussein, a state hockey centre-forward or striker as he would now be called in soccer.

There were only a few girls in Raffles College – perhaps one girl to ten boys. Almost all the girls were Chinese or Eurasian. These communities were a little more advanced than the others in educating their female children up to tertiary level. Parents preferred to keep their daughters at home to learn to cook and excel in domestic duties to please their future husbands. Most parents of all races were keen to marry off their daughters advantageously and not educate them to become career women. Indian and Chinese parents greatly preferred sons to daughters — a tradition the immigrants brought with them from India and China — and usually the sons were given the preference in education. It was even rarer for Malay parents to send their daughters for higher education. When I was teaching in the University of Malaya in Singapore in the late 1950s, I got to know the late Professor of Malay Studies, Zainal Abidin bin Ahmad who was affectionately known as "Za'aba". He told me that he was severely criticised by the Malay community for daring to send his daughters to an English-medium school. It was thought that Malay girls should receive only religious instruction. However, public disapproval did not deter this learned and kindly professor who did what he considered right for his daughters, all of whom did well later in life. I deliberately used the word "kindly" to describe the professor who was my neighbour in Lornie Road. Early one morning I watched him pick up snails from his garden to deposit them outside the hedge from where they eventually returned. When I pointed this out to him he replied, "The poor things are God's creatures too and want to live. Why kill them?"

The credit for the English education of girls and indeed for education generally must go to the Christian missions — American Methodist, Catholic and Anglican. They led the field in both primary and secondary education. The missions received some aid from the colonial government. St Andrew's opened in 1871 and

St Anthony's a few years later. The Anglo-Chinese School began in 1886 and the Methodist Girls' School commenced the following year. Raffles Institution provided secondary education in 1884. It was only in the early years of the 20th century that the government began to build and staff English-medium schools when the demand for schools increased. Chinese schools, supported by the Chinese community, grew up independently and were China-orientated. Years later serious problems arose as a consequence of this, which the leaders of independent Singapore had to resolve.

The girls in Raffles College were popular and received a lot of attention from the adolescent boys who were beginning to be conscious of feminine beauty. This natural development had its comic aspects as, for instance, when one of my friends became entranced by the grace and beauty of a lovely young lady who cast a magic spell on him. The handsome lad, intelligent and personable, practically became her slave, carrying her books to class, taking down lecture notes for her when she was absent and even planning some of her essays for her. We boys at 18 or 19 years of age were dewy-eyed romantics, innocent and naive and all too ready to be swept off our feet whereas up till the age of 15, we had avoided females as we considered them unworthy of our attention. By the time we were in college, most girls were transformed into angels in our imagination. I didn't escape the tender trap either but I am not going to give you any details. First love is lyrical, "all a wonder and a wild desire". What I felt was expressed beautifully by the 17th-century poet John Donne,

> All other things to their destruction draw,
> Only our love hath no decay.
> This no tomorrow hath, nor yesterday,
> Running it never runs from us away,
> But keep his first, last, everlasting day.

One of the best aspects of life in Raffles College was the easy mixing and camaraderie of boys and girls of different races. This was the result of an English education. The situation was very different in the city where a Chinese girl, seen in the company of a non-Chinese, was subject to hostile stares and rude remarks from Chinese males. I think the Chinese were even more racialist than the English — at least in those days. Inter-racial marriages were rare. Even in the 1950s an Indian teacher friend of mine who wished to marry a Chinese girl was not only subjected to parental opposition but death threats! As a boy in Ipoh, an incident happened that illustrates the sense of racial superiority of the Chinese who refer to other races as "devils" classified into black, red-haired or mixed, etc. I was cycling along Chung Thye Pin Road when a young Chinese, standing on his doorstep, called out to me without any provocation, "Hey you! Father horse, mother donkey."

The Students' Union organised annual picnics to offshore islands as well as annual dances. One year we spent an enjoyable day on Pulau Senang where there was a private bungalow and wide stretches of beach of crisp white sand. Picnic lunch with plenty of aerated fizzy drinks from the Fraser and Neave, Phoenix and Framroz companies were available. The last two are no longer in existence. We hired cabin cruisers and launches to take us to Pulau Senang and back. The island later became a penal colony where at one time, the prisoners murdered their wardens and were subsequently put on trial and hanged. I believe it is now used exclusively by our armed forces. The return journey late in the evening was the best part of the picnic as we sang happily together when we approached the harbour. There was a popular song called "Harbour Lights" which was rendered by our best singers to the accompaniment of guitars. We were a happy lot with not a care in the world, although war clouds were darkening over our heads.

Chapter 10

War in Europe

The war in Europe began on 1 September 1939 when Hitler's forces smashed into Poland. On the 3rd, Neville Chamberlain, the Prime Minister of England, declared war on Germany as did France. Gathered round a small radio, we listened to Chamberlain's doom-laden voice. Initial excitement and fears vanished fast as nothing seemed to happen; so we carried on with our studies. The war was too far away and too unreal for us even in 1940 and 1941 when tensions began to build up in the Pacific. It was business as usual in the city and studies as usual in Raffles College. British rule immunised us from feeling any direct involvement and even when the German blitzkrieg inflicted a disastrous defeat on France and the Allied Forces, we were enthralled by the brilliant British evacuation of half a million soldiers from Dunkirk. British propaganda seemed to transform an overwhelming military disaster into some sort of triumph. It all sounded heroic and we never doubted that ultimate victory would be won by Britain. We had been brought up on English history which showed time and again that Britain might lose a battle or two but always won the final battle (except the war with the American colonies). While the British civil servants, bankers and businessmen played cricket on the *padang*, danced in Raffles Hotel and dined in their exclusive Tanglin Club, the Japanese were busily infiltrating Malaya and Singapore as photographers, barbers, dentists, doctors and shopkeepers. In fact, both my dentists in Ipoh and Singapore were Japanese. There was even a vegetable gardener in Cameron Highlands who turned out to be Major Goto in the Nippon Imperial Forces which conquered Malaya and Singapore. The Japanese shops in Middle Road were cheap and well-patronised until the Chinese organised a complete boycott of Japanese goods, even to the extent of using secret society gangsters to beat up any Chinese seen entering a Japanese shop. This happened after the Japanese invasion of China. A China Relief Fund was set afloat to help China. When Singapore fell, the Japanese avenged themselves by a massacre of thousands of young Chinese men.

We were complacent like the British, believing as we did that Singapore was an impregnable fortress. We were told that the Japanese planes were inferior to the Brewster Buffaloes, which were discarded American naval planes acquired for our defence. Time was to prove that the plane was indeed a clumsy buffalo compared to the swift manoeuvring Japanese Zero fighters! We were told that the squint-eyed, shortsighted Japanese pilots would be no match for the English and Australian pilots. If the best British aircraft like the Spitfire and the Hurricane, which matched and defeated the Messersmitts of Germany, had been available, the British pilots would have had a better chance against the Japanese. But these planes were needed to defend a desperate Britain, so the Japanese destroyed the Brewster Buffaloes in aerial combat with the greatest of ease. I saw two of these outdated planes shot down even as they climbed slowly to meet the Japanese fighters which swooped down on them. It was like a swift falcon striking a pigeon in mid-air. I stood in one of the trenches on the Raffles College grounds watching the dogfight. This was in December 1941, but in 1939 and 1940 we Raffles Collegians read our books, wrote our essays and passed our examinations, while continuing to visit Japanese dentists and photographers, patronising Japanese shops where the salesmen bowed low courteously to welcome us, as we smiled a superior smile at the "Made in Japan" trademark. This trademark was a sure sign of inferiority before the war. The best goods came from the United Kingdom and Germany. Japan's exports were usually cheap imitations which had no lasting quality. We led normal everyday lives, blissfully unaware of the fate awaiting us in the hands of Japan between 1942 and 1945.

The final examinations were held in February–March of every year and the one I sat for was in 1941. When the results were published, I was one of two or three fortunate ones who were awarded First Class Diplomas. This led me to apply for the Queen's Scholarship (named after Queen Victoria). These scholarships had been competed for by the brightest schoolboys and girls who sat for a special examination set and marked by Cambridge University. There were three scholarships, two were open and one was specially reserved for the Malays. One scholarship was available in Malaya and one for the Straits Settlements (Penang, Malacca and Singapore). The scholarships entitled the winners to study in Oxford or Cambridge. The amount awarded was £500 for the first year and £400 for subsequent years of whatever course of study chosen by the successful candidate. This amount in pre-war days was a handsome sum as £1 was worth $8.50. As from 1938, the scholarship was transferred to Raffles College and the Medical College graduates with additional two Queen's Fellowships for postgraduate studies. The Queen's Scholarships could be the equivalent of the Rhodes Scholarship or perhaps the President's Scholarships offered by Singapore to its top students to go to Oxford or Cambridge University.

The colonial government limited the number to only two open scholarships as it was not keen about sending too many local students abroad to acquire degrees since the top positions in the civil service were reserved entirely for the whites. The British firms and banks also practised the same policy. Besides, some of the British civil servants, like inspectors of schools, were themselves underqualified and it would not do to have too many local graduates of English universities in the country. Higher education would lead to discontentment and pressures for better jobs and even equality of treatment. While in London, I met a retired Senior Inspector of Schools from Malaya who was appointed as the Warden of Malaya Hall. He was a crude and even ignorant character who had read very little and probably understood even less. The colonial government did not encourage bright local teachers to acquire external degrees by making it clear that they would receive no pay increases. The late Francis Thomas, a Welshman from Cambridge University who taught in St Andrew's School and later became its principal, mentions in his *Memoirs of a Migrant* that he was paid $400 in 1934 when he began teaching with only a degree and no teaching diploma. The most senior teacher in St Andrew's, an able Chinese, received much less! It was not merit or experience that mattered in those days but the colour of one's skin. Francis Thomas later became the Minister for Communications and Works in the short-lived Labour Front administration of David Marshall. When I was engaged as a temporary teacher in 1946 in Choon Guan English School (now the Presbyterian Boys' School) in Koon Seng Road, I was paid a basic salary of $150 and $15 extra for the teaching diploma.

Most of us who graduated in 1941 and were not state scholars from Malaya (each state gave scholarships to selected Malay students) registered for the diploma course in education. A few who preferred not to teach went into the private sector which was very limited in scope then. Two of my friends joined banks but both eventually resigned. I had been awarded an open Raffles College scholarship at the end of my second year so I was not bonded. I registered for the diploma course which would qualify me to teach. I didn't really expect to complete this course when I was awarded the Queen's Scholarship which meant that 1 would leave by boat for England about the middle of 1942.

According to the College regulations, I had to leave the hostel to look for private accommodation in town in my fourth year as the hostel cubicles were reserved for the undergraduates of the first three years. Two good friends, Cheong Weng Choong and the late Robert Ho Guan Hai and I found rooms in a boarding house called "Sophia Home" which was at the top end of Sophia Road next to the Church of England Zenana Mission School (CEZMS). It was also near to the Istana Negara which was then the British High Commissioner's residence. We could walk along Sophia Road into Wilkie Road by a path, with the CEZMS wall sheltering its girls' school on the one side and the fenced, hedged and guarded grounds of the Istana on the other.

As our meals in the boarding house were inadequate, we often walked down to the Rendezvous Restaurant at the junction of Selegie and Bras Basah Roads where for 30 cents, we could enjoy a hearty meal of *nasi padang*! A four-course English meal at the Hai Chin or Mui Chin restaurants in North Bridge Road cost $1.20. A vegetarian meal at an Indian restaurant cost 30 cents for which you could have as many helpings as you wished. A satisfying Chinese dinner at the Albert Street hawker stall cost no more than a dollar or so. It never occured to us to step into Raffles Hotel or the Adelphi Hotel which we believed to be exclusively for Europeans like the Tanglin Club and the Singapore Cricket Club. None of us felt any resentment about exclusive clubs at that time. It was only later, and especially after the overwhelming defeat of the British forces by the Japanese, that we began to question the exclusiveness of such places. I recall that when we were students in London, one of my friends — who later became a minister in independent Singapore — remarking causally in his usual matter-of-fact manner that someone should throw a bomb into the Tanglin Club. Now that the club has opened its doors to all races like the rest of the clubs in Singapore, neither of us bothered to join it!

We believed that the British were fully prepared to defend Malaya and Singapore. We were to discover to our cost that they were not. No air-raid shelters were built but machine-gun emplacements in reinforced concrete appeared in the Pasir Panjang as well as the Bedok and Changi areas. Barbed wire entanglements along the beaches also became visible but, unfortunately, not in the north opposite Johor. The British did not expect or prepare for an attack on Singapore from the north which exactly suited the Japanese strategic plan. The Medical Auxiliary Service (MAS) was organised and some ARP (Air Raid Precautions) wardens were appointed but there were no public air-raid shelters. An excuse was offered that deep shelters were not practicable in low-lying Singapore, as these would be flooded and even breed mosquitoes. Thousands died needlessly as a result of the bombing because there were no shelters. But some wise citizens had built private air-raid shelters for their families.

Chapter 11

The Japanese Invasion

This cataclysmic event changed the lives and shaped the destiny of my generation. Although signs of the approaching catastrophe were there, we were nevertheless taken by surprise when the blow fell. We were as little prepared for the reality of the invasion as the British who had hoodwinked us and themselves too. Though we had news in early December 1941 that Japanese troop transport ships had been sighted off French Indochina (Vietnam) which was under Japanese control after the fall of France, the first air raid on Singapore on the night of 8 December was a shock. All the city lights were on at 4 am although there had been some black-out practices. In any case, the moon shone brightly that night. Singapore's defenders had been caught asleep at their posts. When the sirens sounded, the attacking planes were already leaving. We came out of our rooms in Sophia Home and looked up at the night sky. Lim Kean Siew, now a leading lawyer in Penang, who was living with us then, pointed at the night sky where three silver streaks were clearly etched out in the moonlight. These were the last three of the departing squadron, the rest of which were invisible.

We heard the drone of the departing raiders. The anti-aircraft batteries opened up but only after the crash of bombs in the distance. We hurried downstairs to take cover. We tried desperately to wake up Robert Ho who was a heavy sleeper but we failed. The next morning he accused us of heartlessly abandoning him. In fact we had dragged him out of his bed shouting, "Jap planes, Jap planes bombing," but he had just flopped back into bed!

Early in the morning, we rushed back to Raffles College to report for duty in the MAS. I was a corporal in charge of a unit of six which included Lee Kuan Yew and Philip Liau, who was to become Principal of Raffles Institution one day. There is hardly any need to say what position the other was to attain! Our duty was to attend to the casualties of enemy air raids and take them to hospital. As we made our way to the college, we noticed that people appeared in groups looking excited and worried. But we saw no sign of panic. Later we learned that Raffles Place had been badly damaged and houses along Killiney Road had been destroyed. There were a lot of casualties in Boat Quay and Market Street. My medical unit was sent to Tiong Bahru where we had to dig up a collapsed earth shelter in which we found a mother with two little children in her arms, all suffocated to death. They need not have died if there had been a proper shelter. We were deeply saddened by this as we were to be later, again and again, by the innocent dead and wounded after each bombing raid. We were told that in the first raid, 60 people had been killed in Raffles Place alone. Shattered glass from the shops lay thick all around. Casualties were heavy in subsequent raids too as the Japanese bombers kept out of the range of the British anti-aircraft guns and the British fighters were never fast enough to tackle the Japanese aircraft. We never saw a single Japanese plane shot down.

The first broadcast we heard on 8 December announced that the Japanese had landed in Kota Baru in Kelantan, 400 miles from Singapore. We were informed too of the devastating attack on the American navy in Pearl Harbour which had destroyed a great many warships and had brought the USA into the war. The news that the United States was now in the war boosted our morale as we could not imagine how the Japanese could ever get the better of the combined Anglo-American forces. How could the Japanese deal with the British navy represented by the HMS *Prince of Wales*, a redoubtable battleship reputed to be unsinkable and the veteran HMS *Repulse*? We found out soon enough to our horror when we were told on 11 December that both these warships, which had set out from Singapore to intercept the Japanese landings in Kota Baru, were sunk by Japanese planes on 10 December. The British fleet met its fate off Kuantan as it had no fighter protection. The Japanese lost only six planes to ack-ack (anti-aircraft) fire in sinking the pride of the British fleet. We realised then that nothing short of a miracle could save Malaya but still had faith in the "impregnable" island fortress of Singapore.

The MAS unit I led did a twelve-hour shift. When we were on night duty, we played cards to keep awake and while away the time. We even tried poker for nominal stakes of a cent or two. We played till dawn when we went off duty to sleep.

Meanwhile, part of the hostel was converted into an emergency hospital to receive survivors of the crew of the *Prince of Wales* and the *Repulse*, many of whom were wounded. One 19-year-old gunner had a bullet through his neck but it missed the vital spot. He was able to give us a firsthand account of the one-sided battle. He did say that the Japanese planes did not machine-gun the survivors in the sea or attack the four destroyers which were attempting to rescue the sailors who were struggling in the water. In the early stages of the war, the Japanese air force and navy displayed some of their much-vaunted bushido spirit. It was reported that the Japanese fliers later threw a wreath into the sea where the *Prince of Wales* and the *Repulse* went down. The Japanese air force and navy behaved better and at times, with chivalry, unlike the army. The Japanese elite joined the navy or the air force whereas the army was mostly made up of peasants including Koreans and Taiwanese. Korea and Taiwan were colonies of Japan before the Pacific war.

While the bombing went on, especially in the dock areas, those of us from Malaya were worried about our families. My mother and father, brother and sister were in Cameron Highlands. When the Japanese broke through the British defence lines in the north and advanced rapidly, the British announced one "strategic withdrawal" after another. We Malayans applied for leave to return home but the college authorities were reluctant to let us go. Most of us decided to leave anyway and took the mail train north. I got off at Tapah and arrived by bus in Camerons to find that my father, along with all Europeans, had been enrolled in the local defence unit which was soon to be evacuated to Singapore as the Japanese juggernaut rolled south. We wanted to leave too but my mother adamantly refused. She decided to stay put to look after my epileptic brother but she urged us to go. Not even terrifying rumours of Japanese-atrocities could change her mind. She insisted that my sister, who was a beautiful girl, should be evacuated to India or Australia and told me to see to it. So my sister and I left the Camerons as the Japanese advanced into Perak with astonishing speed. General Yamashita devised brilliant infiltration tactics by which his troops got behind each defence line and demoralised the defenders who had to withdraw. When we reached Kuala Lumpur (KL) we found it a deserted town, but we managed to find a hotel to stay the night. The next day we managed to secure two berths in the night mail which left KL at 10 pm. Fortunately for us, the railway tracks south of KL had not yet been bombed nor was the train attacked from the air. Two days after we had arrived in Singapore, the Tapah Road station, which served those going to or coming from Cameron Highlands, was bombed and the

Maurice Baker's sister, Margaret, as a young woman.

Margaret, a school girl dressed in a sarong kebaya.

train was strafed. My neighbours in Camerons, an English family of four, were all killed in the attack. They were Mr Battensby, his wife and her aged parents whose house was humorously named "The Belfry" reminding one of the phrase "bats in the belfry". I mention this because their bungalow was said to be haunted by Mrs B's father. Doors and windows would open or close of their own accord and one villager told me that when he tried sleeping in the empty house, he found himself outside at dawn! He claimed to have been thrown out by the ghost! Nobody dared to live in The Belfry. Even after the Communist insurgency of 1948 to 1960 when the house deteriorated into a ruin, it retained its haunted reputation. Eventually a rubber magnate bought the land and reconstructed the house. People who moved in, moved out quickly, claiming that it was still haunted. This new house in turn became a deserted ruin and was eventually demolished. There is now a commercial flower garden on the site, believe it or not!

But to get back to the war, those of us from Malaya who had returned to Singapore reported back to Raffles College. We assembled on the lower quadrangle of the Bukit Timah Campus where one of the British science lecturers insulted us, calling us traitors. This almost led to a nasty incident as I stepped out to hit him. Fortunately the situation was saved by cooler heads amongst us. I should like to mention Tun Haji Hamdan bin Sheikh Tahir, who later became Vice-Chancellor, Universiti Sains Malaysia and eventually Governor of Penang, and Tun Syed Zahirudin who held me back and perhaps saved me from jail. The lecturer, who was a diabetic, died in internment. Looking back on what happened, I suppose he was under a great strain, fearful for his future, and so perhaps he lashed out at us to relieve his feelings.

The Raffles College medical auxiliary units were kept busy attending to casualties due to the increasing number of Japanese raids. The enemy aircraft raided in broad daylight, usually in a formation of 27 planes which were clearly visible, though flying too high for our ack-ack (anti-aircraft) guns. There were no British fighters to intercept the attackers. Sometimes I was told to do some roof-spotting for Raffles College to keep a look-out for the raiders. Only once did the bombs fall on the college grounds. I think these were stray bombs which missed the buildings. One fell near Professor Dyer's house. It did not do much damage, merely creating a large hole in the ground. No one was hurt. The bombers unloaded their deadly cargo on military installations on the airfield, on the docks and Chinatown. I suspect the Japanese deliberately made Chinatown a target because they hated the Chinese.

It was a sad job collecting the badly injured and looking at the dead, but occasionally there were odd amusing incidents. Once we saw a large pig on the edge of a huge bomb crater, its hindquarters buried in mud but very much alive and kicking. We set it free. When the Japanese reached Johor and began shelling Singapore before landing, we had to endure both the bombing and the whine of the shells overhead and the explosion when they hit a target. Once after a heavy bombing raid on Bukit Panjang village about the 10th milestone on Bukit Timah Road, Professor Dyer assembled the MAS units and asked for volunteers to go on a rescue mission to Bukit Panjang. As the shelling was going on, it was, he said, a dangerous mission. Lee Kuan Yew and I were among the six who stepped forward to proceed there in a Singapore Traction Company bus which had been converted into a makeshift ambulance. The village was in flames and there were huge craters on the road which the driver had to steer around cautiously. We walked into a rubber estate where some bombs had fallen. The fins of an unexploded bomb roused the curiosity of a member of our group who wanted to investigate it. I had to restrain him from his recklessness. We found no casualties in the rubber estate but later we came across an injured Chinese girl with a shrapnel wound in her groin. Kuan Yew gave her first-aid under my supervision. All of us returned to Raffles College without any mishap.

An incident in those days, just before the capitulation of Singapore, is firmly etched in my memory. My MAS unit came on duty at 8 am on the morning of 31 January 1942. I was talking to our former Prime Minister, who as I said belonged to the same unit. He was leaning against the parapet in the corridor of the Oei Tiong Ham Building, which was the administrative block. Professor W E Dyer, the principal, was coming down the corridor towards us on his way to his office. Suddenly the whole island was shaken by a thunderous explosion. We were stunned. Dyer stood still for a second before coming nearer toward us. Lee Kuan Yew exclaimed, "That is the end of the British Empire!" It was indeed! Dyer passed on as if he had not heard it. But I am sure he did. It was the sound of the causeway linking Malaya and Singapore being blown up by the beaten British forces when all resistance to the Japanese had ended on the mainland. A gap of about 60 yards was made on the Johor side and so began the seige of Singapore which was to last a mere week. General Percival who commanded the British forces surrendered to General Yamashita on 15 February, Chinese New Year's day. If he had fought on, he would have inflicted untold sufferings on the civilian population, swollen by refugees from the north, who had already reached the limits of their endurance. The water supply failed. Daily bombing raids and continuous shelling had damaged the pipes so the water ran to waste.

We had followed the course of the battle in the Malay Peninsula with increasing dismay throughout December and January. Whenever the British, Australian and Indian defenders put up a defence line as at Slim River or Muar, the Japanese troops infiltrated behind the defences either through jungle paths or along the coast by boats they had captured in Penang. The British, in their panic to escape from Penang, had failed to destroy the boats which proved to be useful to the Japanese. The defenders were bewildered by the speed and tactics of the invaders. The Japanese soldiers proved to be courageous and adept at jungle fighting, able to survive by foraging, carrying cooked rice in bamboo containers and riding on requisitioned bicycles. The Japanese rode on bicycles instead of horses. They improvised effectively whereas the British had to truck different supplies for their white and Indian troops. The trunk roads were often jammed and easy targets for the Japanese pilots. The British had no tanks to counter the small but fast Japanese tanks because they believed that the tank would not be effective on Malayan terrain. Many years after the war, I learned from Japanese accounts of their campaign in Malaya how surprised they had been at the speed of their advance and the weakness of the defenders. Inadequately trained and badly led, the mixed British forces were no match for the battle-hardened Japanese who had fought in China. It was not the lack of courage on the part of the British soldier but the lack of experience, the lack of air support and the inability to counter the unorthodox infiltration tactics of the enemy that brought about the disaster. The Japanese conquered Malaya in sixty days and took Singapore in seven days.

Chapter 12

The Fall of Singapore

When the siege of Singapore began on 1 February, there were still many of us who believed in the myth of "Fortress Singapore", the "Gibraltar of the East" and that the island would be another defiant Malta. Malta, in the Mediterranean Sea, had withstood German bombing for years. We were aware that huge quantities of food had been stored up and that troop reinforcements were on the way. The more realistic among us perhaps had little hope when we saw the beaten and bedraggled troops retreat to Singapore. The sinking of the *Prince of Wales* and the *Repulse* had already demoralised the civilians right at the beginning of the Japanese onslaught. No doubt the British troops were even more demoralised by a succession of defeats they suffered as they withdrew from one defence line to the next down the Malay Peninsula. Now they had to face the triumphant Japanese who were brimming with confidence as they prepared to invade Singapore. The end was inevitable. It was merely a matter of time. But human beings usually live in hope of better things. As Alexander Pope, the 18th-century English poet wrote, "Hope springs eternal in the human breast, Man never is, but always to be blest." Some of us prayed for a miracle to save us but miracle there was none.

I was on duty every day with the medical auxiliary unit. Most of us slept in Raffles College in the adjoining bungalows once used by members of the staff. The main building was used as an emergency hospital as I have already mentioned.

The Japanese began shelling Singapore in early February. This was a new experience for us after we had got used to the drone of enemy planes and the eerie whistling sound of the bombs before the explosions which followed. We even got used to the sight of low-flying Zero fighters. One night, when I was off duty and preparing for bed, I heard a double "thud, thud" of firing in the distance. Then there was a whining screech of piercing intensity as the shell passed overhead on its way to its target. An explosion followed. This was a nerve-racking experience as there was no siren to warn us, nor was there an all clear long blast of the siren when an air raid was over. The shelling was unpredictable. It was continuous for an hour or so, then it would stop. Soon it started again. The shells from Johor screeched over Raffles College on their way to the city. No shell actually hit the Raffles College buildings.

The medical auxiliary units based in Raffles College were disbanded on 11 or 12 February, as far as I can recall. Two of my friends and I walked into the shattered city, which looked abandoned and derelict and took refuge in the St Joseph's School building for a night. Then we moved into the house of the Holmberg family in Queen Street. One of the three brothers in the family was my contemporary in Raffles College, so we were welcomed by them. The only shelter we had was under the staircase of the two-storey terrace house opposite the Portuguese Catholic Church. Twice we came close to being killed by shells. One shell fell right in front of the house in the monsoon drain. It was a dud! The second shell hit the back wall of the house. I was then in the kitchen at the back with one of the Holmbergs cooking some rice and sardines. The kitchen was protected by a second wall. A whole basket of live ducks was buried under the rubble of the demolished wall but they scuttled away, dazed but alive to quack another day. A bomb scored a direct hit on Ichigoya, a Japanese shop on Middle Road which was close to us. We were sheltering under the staircase. The house shook and the pictures tumbled from the walls in a cloud of dust. We thought the house would collapse on us but it withstood the blast. The good ladies of the house, praying under the staircase with rosaries in hand, thanked God for our survival.

We had moved out of Raffles College only when the Japanese troops, which had landed on the night of 8 February on the north-west coast of Singapore, penetrated into Bukit Panjang village. We could hear the rat-tat-tat of the machine guns at night and fearfully expected to be confronted by Japanese soldiers at any moment. A blanket of darkness from the smoke of burning oil dumps at the naval base spread over the city. The British had set these oil dumps on fire to prevent them from falling into enemy hands. Black rain fell, each drop saturated with soot. Thick columns of black smoke continued to rise and shroud the skies. The pall of smoke turned the day into night. English, Indian and Australian soldiers, dispirited, battle-weary and lost, roamed the streets. In Bencoolen Street, I saw a white soldier draw his revolver and fire at the bolted gate of a Chinese bakery. A crowd was outside waiting for bread which was rationed. When the bolts were shattered, the mob rushed into the shop to grab as many loaves as possible. It was chaotic. Many were hurt. I saw the Commonwealth soldiers lying in drains, firing their guns at low-flying Japanese planes which machine-gunned them. I ran for cover. Looters were active after every raid until the Japanese took over the city and executed those they caught on the spot. Wrecked and abandoned cars were all over the city. In Middle Road and Dhoby Ghaut, the telephone wires were down, twisted and burnt-out metal lay everywhere. Corpses lay on the streets along with dead cats and dogs awaiting burial. The stench was unbearable. A severed leg, still in its soldier's boot, lay in front of the Cathay Building where the cinema had continued to show films till the last few days. The building was full of weary and worn-out Australian soldiers, who had borne the brunt of the fighting on the island. An Indian soldier showed me his water container neatly punctured by a Japanese bullet. He shook his head and tapped his chest as he talked of his narrow escape from the battlefront. The civilian defence corps, including those who had been evacuated from up-country, were housed in the Cathay Building. It was here that I saw my father again and said goodbye for the last time until after the surrender of the Japanese in August 1945. He was interned in Changi and later in the Sime Road camp. The Cathay Building escaped damage though the Orchard Road area was heavily bombed. On the whole, the Japanese concentrated their bombing on military targets as well as the wharves and docks, but they also vented their fury on Chinatown where there was no military installation. The crowded shophouses were death-traps and casualties were horrific. As Japan was at war with China, the Japanese probably regarded all overseas Chinese, no matter how innocent, as their enemies.

It was a shell probably aimed at Chinatown which killed a group of medical undergraduates in the General Hospital grounds. They had gathered together for the funeral of a fellow student who had been fatally injured in an earlier air raid. As they were burying their friend, a shell exploded near them, killing all, including a good friend of mine, Hera Singh, who was the Medical College's best cricketer. They were all buried in a mass grave, along with other civilians, where they fell, together with the one whose last rites they had so loyally attended. Other friends of mine from Raffles College who were murdered by the Japanese include

Fam Pau Onn, Chew Kong Fong, Seah Yun Hien and Oh Swee Kia who were picked at random because they were well-built young men during the security screening of all Chinese after the fall of Singapore.

> They shall grow not old, as we that are left
>   grow old:
> Age shall not weary them, nor the years
>   condemn;
> At the going down of the sun, and in the
>   morning
> We shall remember them.
>
> (Lawrence Binyon, *For the Fallen*)

They take their place with the rest of the men and women of all nationalities, soldiers and civilians alike who were killed in the Second World War (1939–1945).

We, the survivors in Singapore, knew the end of the seige was near when the water taps began to run dry. We filled every bath tub, every container and bottle and rationed ourselves. We denied ourselves the luxury of baths. Water was for drinking and cooking only. The main source of supply from Johor was cut off, but this had been anticipated. Singapore's three reservoirs at the time, it was thought, could have supplied the 17 or so million gallons needed daily after measures had been taken to reduce consumption. But the population of Singapore had doubled to more than a million with the influx of refugees from the mainland and the 100,000 troops. During the last days, the reservoirs were captured by the Japanese but in any case, many of the mains and pipes had been damaged in the bombing and the precious water was wasted.

The situation worsened and the more desperate it became, the greater were the optimistic rumours. We were told that the Americans had landed at Mersing and/or Batu Pahat; that the

Japanese were cut off in Johor; that swarms of allied planes would blacken the skies soon. Every defeat and "strategic withdrawal" through December and January brought wild rumours of hope. Who originated these rumours I never knew but they did keep alive the hopes of many. One of the Holmbergs had a small radio which unfortunately failed during the last crucial days. So all we heard were the rumours while the shells whined overhead and the bombs exploded around us. In the worst of times, when facing calamity, human beings seem capable of creating and believing illusions which keep up their hopes. When the guns suddenly fell silent on the night of 15 February, the terrified dogs which had stopped barking for a week, all at once barked again. It was an eerie night. I knew that the British had surrendered but even on that night of despair, there was the absurd hopeful whisper that it was the Japanese who had surrendered! The fall of Singapore was in the words of Winston Churchill, "the worst disaster and the largest capitulation in British history".

It was a night of fear. What horrors would tomorrow bring? We woke up on the morning of 16 February to see a huge flag of the rising sun, blood-red circle on white, at the top of Cathay Building — the highest in Singapore in 1942. Singapore had died in battle. Syonan was born. It was the saddest day of my life. My friend, Chin, and I decided to walk towards the Cathay Building. We picked our way through the rubble and the shell holes, past the twisted metal of abandoned cars and trucks, over fallen telegraph poles and wires, unable to avoid the stench of dead dogs and cats and grotesque corpses in the ditches. The dead lay all around us in a city torn apart by war, shattered by bombs and shells. We did not get very far nor did we expect to. A Japanese sentry stood outside the Cathay Building rifle in hand, with naked bayonet gleaming. He yelled at us, the only two foolhardy men in sight. We approached him in fear. He rattled off in Japanese but he pointed at me and said, *"Maraiyul"* which I guessed meant "Malay". I nodded vigorously. He looked at Chin and recognised that he was Chinese. He growled at him and yelled, *"Kora, kora"* pointing the bayonet menacingly at his stomach. He then waved me on and pointed at Chin to turn back. I longed to double back too but didn't dare. So I walked on into Orchard Road. Chin turned back of course, thankful to be alive.

I saw four truckloads of unshaven but jaunty Japanese soldiers in their cloth caps, some grinning, entering the city. They were followed by commandeered Singapore Traction Company buses, also laden with the triumphant troops. They looked so small and unimpressive. I wondered how these little men could have mangled the Commonwealth army beyond recognition. These short men were mighty conquerors. I walked on slowly up Orchard Road to the old Cold Storage building, now Centrepoint. There was a barricade across the street. I decided to push my luck no further and made my way back briskly to Queen Street. Chin was safely back too. What our eyes had seen dispelled all false hopes. This was defeat. What of the future? The Holmbergs wondered how long we would be under the Japanese sword. Strange as it may seem none of us believed that the Japanese victory would be permanent. How many months? A year perhaps? The most pessimistic among us put it at two years. But our immediate worry was how the enemy troops would behave. Stories of rape and rapine in Malaya and Hong Kong terrified the women who hid from the invaders in the attics and other supposedly safe places. Fortunately General Yamashita decided to protect Singapore from the massacres suffered by some cities in China like Nanking. He sent in the military police ahead of the army and limited the movement of the soldiers. Apparently he had guaranteed General Percival at the surrender that women and children and civilians would be safe. We learnt this later when our worst fears of pillage proved unfounded.

There was some looting of provision shops and abandoned bungalows in many areas but the Japanese promptly put an end to this. They executed those they caught in the act and exhibited the severed heads on poles as a warning to all. The looting stopped. Such drastic punishment frightened thieves and robbers into behaving themselves throughout the occupation. I picked up a pamphlet signed by General Yamashita, who came to be known as the "Tiger of Malaya", which threatened that all looters and traitors who disobeyed the orders of the Nippon army would be "severely punished". This, we soon realised, meant summary execution. Specific mention was made of spies, those who committed "rebellious acts" or any act to injure anyone in the Nippon army, and those who destroyed the railways, cables and telephones. Curiously enough, potential poisoners were also warned against "spreading any poison or bacteria" to harm the Nippon army — perhaps the Japanese troops had suffered from poisoned wells in China.

The list of offences was enlarged in a newspaper, the *Syonan Times* which appeared on 20 February at 5 cents a copy in the form of a single sheet. On the back of the page was a "Declaration of the Commander of the Nippon Army" in bold print. The front page carried the headline that Japan's position had become impregnable with the fall of Singapore. There were four columns of news items and the editorial announcing that the press had come "under the domination of Nippon troops" and that the Commander wished to preserve "the civilization (*sic*) of the people" and to ensure that "the policy of injustice, unrighteousness and cunning shall disappear automatically just as the smoke of the burning Fortress is in fact disappearing". A "New Order" would take the place of the old. There were half a dozen pleas for lost members of families to return home. Essential workers in gas, electricity, waterworks and broadcasting were ordered to report for duty. People were urged to clean the streets and compounds of their houses. Very soon, the captured white troops and European civilians were forced to do these menial tasks in order to humiliate them.

As a matter of interest, I reproduce here exactly with all its peculiarities, the declaration, as both the content and the stilted style are amusing though never meant to be so:

DECLARATION
OF THE
COMMANDER OF THE NIPPON ARMY

Singapore is not only the connective pivot of the British Empire to control British India, Australia and EAST ASIA, but the strong base to invade and squeeze them and Britain has boasted of its impregnable features for many years and it is generally accepted as an unsurmountable fortress.

Since the Nippon armies, however, have taken a military operation over the Malay Peninsula and Singapore, they have overwhelmed the whole peninsula within only two months and smashed the strong fort to pieces within 7 days and thus the British dominating power in British India, Australia and East Asia has collapsed in a moment and changed to, as if, a fan without a rivet or an umbrella without a handle.

Originally, the English has entertained extremely egoistic and dogmatic principles and they not only have despised other, but have been accustomed to carry out the foxy, deceit, cunning and intimidation and they dared to commit the injustice and unrighteousness in order to keep only their own interest, and thus they have really spoiled the whole world.

Now, considering from the military proceeding of the Nippon Army and in view of the British administrations and their results, the traces of the British squeeze on Malayans are very clear and the British Armies, during their operations and also on retreating from the front, have confiscated and looted the treasures, properties, provisions and resources from the populace and sent them backward for destruction and dared to throw the people into severe pains by burning their houses and also they placed the Indian and Australian troops on the front while the English troops, remaining in Singapore, had the former at their back. Thus the English egoism, injustice and unrighteousness are beyond description and worthy to be called as the common enemy of humanity.

The reason why Nippon has stood up resolutely this time, taking her sword of evil-breaking, is very clear as already explained in several declarations of the Nippon Government and it is needless to declare again. We, however, hope that we sweep away the arrogant and unrighteous British elements and share pain and rejoicing with all concerned peoples in a spirit of "give and take", and also hope to promote the social development by establishing the East Asia Co-prosperity Sphere on which the New Order of Justice have to be attained under "the Great Spirit of Cosmocracy" giving all content to the respective race and individual according to their talents and faculties. So, Nippon Army will hereafter endeavour further to sweep out the remaining power of Britain and U.S.A. from the adjoining regions and intend to realize the external developments and policies of Malaya after curing the wound caused by British bloody squeeze in the long time past and restoring the war damage inflicted in this war.

Nippon armies hereby wish Malayan people to understand the real intention of Nippon and to co-operate with Nippon army toward the prompt establishment of the New Order and the Co-prosperity Sphere. Nippon army will drastically expel and punish those who still pursue bended delusions as heretofore, those who indulge themselves in private interests and wants, those who act against humanity or disturb the public order and peace and those who are against the orders and disturb the military action of Nippon Army.

On the fall of Singapore, the above declarations have hereby been given to the populace to indicate the right way for the purpose of eliminating their possible mistakes.

Tomoyuki Yamashita
The Commander of Nippon Army
February, 1942.

I rather like the colloquial sound of "British bloody squeeze" which became a favourite phrase of the Japanese press when referring to the British exploitation of their colonies. The Japanese, with complete disregard of the irony of the situation, proceeded to squeeze the Chinese community as hard as they could by demanding "voluntary contributions" of 50 million dollars. This was an impossible sum to raise at that time and some of the money had to be borrowed from the Yokohama Bank. I suppose the Japanese must have enjoyed themselves punishing the Chinese for their regular aid to China over the years in its struggle against the Japanese and for the effective boycott of Japanese goods and shops. Readers will notice the original imagery of British power becoming "a fan without a rivet" and "an umbrella without a handle". This curious phraseology is no doubt the result of a literal translation of Japanese into English. The umbrella image is certainly effective although one could just place the umbrella on one's head and wear it like a huge hat!

This declaration appeared on three successive days. It was followed by a notification listing the controlled prices of foodstuffs. This was necessary as no one knew what prices to charge or to pay for the daily necessities. I remember a *yu char kway* hawker on Middle Road selling a piece for 5 cents though the normal price was 2 cents. I bought a few for the Holmbergs and eagerly ate one on the way back. British currency was in use but in short supply. Soon the

Japanese issued their "banana" dollars which multiplied like rice beetles in a sack of grain. Japanese currency rapidly diminished in value. The administration threatened severe punishment for profiteers. Here are some of the controlled prices: Beef — 45 cents a kati; lean pork — 60 cents a kati; chicken — 50 cents a kati; duck — 30 cents; *ikan kurau* — 65 cents a kati. Very little fresh food was on sale but mounds of tinned goods such as corned beef and condensed milk appeared on the roadsides. A lot of these tins had been given away by the British army in the last days before the surrender but some had also been looted. Sardines and condensed milk were sold at 10 cents a tin and a whole case of 48 tins of corned beef was available for $3! Soon speculators moved in and cornered the stocks so that within weeks, the prices soared on the black market. Thai rice which sold at 6 cents per kati in the last days of British rule, was retailed at 200 Japanese dollars by 1944. But by then, inflation was sky-high and the Japanese currency was almost worthless. By 1945 condensed milk and corned beef had become priceless delicacies. I carefully kept a tin of corned beef to celebrate a very special occasion — the surrender of the Japanese in August 1945. Food shortages grew in severity, especially in the towns, once the rice stored up by the British was consumed. People had to live on sweet potatoes (which I like), tapioca and corn bread. Wheat flour was unavailable so bread disappeared for the duration of the war. Imagine — no rice and no bread! Not even the black market could offer bread at any price. We forgot the taste of bread and butter till after the war. A loaf of corn bread was so hard that it could be used as a missile! One needed a good set of teeth to chew a slice of this bread.

The *Syonan Times* was the propaganda medium for the Japanese. It was naive at times, especially in its extravagant claims of famous victories over the Allied Forces. It is true though that in the first six months of 1942, the Japanese rapidly conquered Burma, the

Philippines and the south-west Pacific islands. But the Japanese naval superiority ended at the battle of the Midway Island in June 1942 when four of their aircraft-carriers were sunk. However they went on claiming victory after victory in battle after battle on land and sea, always inflicting tremendous losses on their opponents while suffering slight damage themselves. Soon nobody believed their reports. Occasionally I found an amusing report to cheer me up. I remember an article entitled "Heaven's Retribution for British Audacity" which claimed that the British believed that each white baby was endowed with a God-given right to rule over seven coloured races. Why seven? No explanation. It spoke of the British "haughtily" subjugating Malaya "with their wild nature", deceiving the people and occupying the country "just like a hungry lion hunts a deer". It then went on to describe how the Nippon Volunteer Corp and the navy helped to suppress the Indian mutiny in Singapore in 1915. The writer then must have been somewhat embarrassed by this fact as the Japanese were encouraging the Indians to form the Indian National Army to help them conquer India. So he explained that Nippon helping the British was really an act of God! The defeat of the British was said to be divine retribution for Britain's audacious baby claim.

On the whole, the news was uniformly grim on the battlefronts in the weeks that followed the fall of Singapore. The Japanese navy claimed to have annihilated the combined British–Dutch naval force in the battle of the Java Sea within a fortnight of Singapore's surrender. Soon the Netherlands East Indies (now Indonesia) was captured by the Japanese. It was only in the Philippines, in Bataan and Corregidor that the fight continued a little longer. This was because the Filipinos fought heroically side by side with the Americans who had trained and trusted them with arms. Despite the obvious successes of the Japanese forces, rumour-mongers continued to land British and American forces at various points in the Malay Peninsula and Java. The Japanese air force, navy and army seemed invincible in early 1942. For us in Singapore, it was a question of survival, the need to find food and to avoid getting in the way of the Japanese troops. Toyo Hotel on Queen Street, right next door to the Holmberg house, became a centre for Japanese officers. It had been a Japanese hotel before. An armed sentry stood guard outside the hotel so the moment we stepped out of the house, we had to come to attention and bow low to him. This had to be repeated on our return. Every sentry had to be bowed to. Anyone who failed to do so was instantly slapped across the face. If you should be riding a bicycle, you had to get off and bow. Sometimes the sentry would punish an offender by making him stand at attention holding a large stone over his head for an hour or for as long as he thought fit. Every sentry was a law unto himself and did as he pleased. We were quick to learn our lesson in Japanese courtesy.

The Chinese community in Singapore suffered the most. Ordered to report at various centres all over the island, the Chinese gathered in their thousands — men, women and even children — standing in the hot sun and the rain while they were screened by the Kempetai with the aid of informers. The Kempetai was a military police force which could arrest civilians and soldiers alike and use torture to extract information. The Kempetai imposed a reign of terror in Singapore. The screening varied at the different centres. Sometimes the women and children and the aged were sent back after a day or two. Thousands of young men who were taken away were never seen again. Later we learned that they were massacred in Changi and off Blakang Mati. Nobody can tell how many Chinese males were shot. The Japanese admitted to having killed 6,000 but the Chinese put the number much higher. The moving tale of one or two survivors of the massacre is told in N I Low's book *When Singapore was Syonan-to* and in a recent publication *The Killer They Called a God* by Ian Ward (1992). The blame for the mass murders is placed squarely on Colonel Masanobu Tsuji who escaped after the Japanese surrender, disguised as a Thai monk and later wrote a book entitled *Singapore: The Japanese Version*.

The Japanese were determined to identify the Chinese volunteers who made up the Dalforce, who were trained hurriedly in the last few weeks by Lt Col Dalley and who fought gallantly with the regular troops. Three Raffles College students joined this force and were fortunate enough to escape the screening. I must also mention the Malay regiment which defended Pasir Panjang with great heroism and while inflicting big losses on the Japanese, also suffered severe casualties. The Japanese executed the Malay officers whom they captured. The courage and determination displayed by the Dalforce and the Malay regiment proved that the British should have had more faith in the local population to defend Singapore as the Americans did in the Philippines.

The Eurasians were the next community to be ordered to report for registration with full details of parentage, profession and whether they were members of the Volunteers, the Police or any department connected with British propaganda. I was one of the early ones to assemble on the Padang in front of the Singapore Recreation Club building. When my turn came to face Mamoru Shinozaki who was in charge, I avoided telling the whole truth. Although I was then a graduate of Raffles College, I put myself down as a clerk as most Eurasians did white-collar jobs. I also claimed that my father was half-Irish when he was in fact English. I guessed that direct descendants would be interned. Shinozaki, a humane and helpful man who had been a diplomat in the Japanese Embassy in Singapore and had been imprisoned by the British as a spy, saved many Chinese by issuing passes to them as he did to us. He was later to write two books, My *Wartime Experiences in Singapore* and *Syonan — My Story* which make interesting reading. The Japanese were under the impression that the Eurasians had been specially favoured by the British, so some of those who were briefly detained were given a severe lecture. A part of this lecture was reported in the *Syonan Times* on 6 March and ran as follows in rather picturesque English but was very sensible at times:

> Until now you were spoiled on circumstances of individualism liberalism. You were used to an easy-going life of amusements but you will soon see the real idea of mankind, the new conception of the New World. The defeat of materialism is proved in the History of the Roman Empire. It is the real object of building up a New Asia to gain the spiritualism you have forgotten entirely. Look!
>
> The burning of the dead lightens up the Syonan sky. The New Dawn has come over a new Great Asia.
>
> Those who emphasize their rights and ideas, forgetting their duties and services, are an evil to the nation ...
>
> If you understand our true object and serve Our Imperial Majesty, we shall take you up as a new Japanese people — that is, we shall accept you as brothers.

Well, I suppose you could say I was accepted as a Japanese brother as I was still alive and I was free by concealing my true parentage.

The European civilians led by the Governor Sir Shenton Thomas had to line up on the esplanade on 23 and 24 February to be marched off to Changi jail. Only those in the essential services such as doctors and engineers were asked to continue in their jobs temporarily until the Japanese civilians arrived to take over getting the city back into gear.

We watched thousands of Commonwealth troops marching past along Queen Street to internment, singing "Glory, Glory, Halleluia" as they went by. There were some of us who wept in sympathy at this moving sight. There were Chinese and other Asians who passed food and water bottles to the marching men, many of whom were destined not to survive the three and a half years of prison and starvation that lay ahead of them. Only the Japanese and a few Indian soldiers, especially the Sikhs, appeared grinning and joyful at the sight of the white men, professors and civil servants sweeping the streets and the drains of the city they had once ruled. Most of us felt a tinge of sorrow for the defeated men, women and children — especially the women and children although the "mems" had been the most arrogant and colour-conscious as in India and elsewhere in the British colonies. We ourselves were destined to be not much better off outside the internment camps and were half-starved too, but at least we could get out of the way of our brutal conquerors. Had the Japanese avoided the cruel mass murders of the Chinese and treated the local population better, they might have earned the co-operation of many fellow Asians. But they lost the opportunity and their oppressive rule made the people long for the return of the more humane British despite their faults.

I had made up my mind to return home to Cameron Highlands as soon as possible as I knew that in wartime the city dwellers would suffer from shortages of food. I also wanted to be where I would encounter as few Japanese as possible and Syonan was certainly not the place.

Chapter 13

Homeward Bound

The time of my return home was decided for me by the Nippon authorities. Chinese refugees from the mainland had been ordered to leave Syonan by road or rail in late February and on 6 March, refugees of all nationalities were commanded to do the same. The order stated frankly that Syonan was overcrowded and that there was an impending shortage of food. It claimed falsely that the Malay Peninsula had been reorganised and would provide a comfortable living. Finally the order stated bluntly that all those who did not leave Syonan by 14 March would be "severely punished". Anyone in doubt quickly made up his mind to go north. We could go by road on foot as there were no buses or cars except for those in the hands of the Japanese. Those who lived in Johor could walk back but for the rest of us, the best way was to go by train. There were only open goods wagons and covered cattle trucks but no passenger coaches for us refugees. Those who decided to go by rail had to obtain permits from the military. The permit was priced according to your race. A Malay had to pay $1;

an Indian $2; all others had to pay $5. The wagon and cattle truck fares were as follows:

> From Syonan to Gemas   : $3.00
> From Syonan to Kuala Lumpur   : $5.00
> From Syonan to Ipoh   : $7.00

The exact amount had to be handed over. No change could be expected at the railway station. Each passenger was told to carry his own food and personal belongings, "which can be carried by one hand only". There was a final note about motor cars:

> Principally no motor-cars (including trucks) are allowed to return to their former places. But if any car owners can produce certification of ownership and has really no potential enmity, the car is allowed to go across the causeway by special permit. The owner shall pay $100 as tariff.

As almost all the cars that had escaped the bombing and the shelling had been confiscated, as petrol was hard to come by, and as anyone with a $100 to spare could be considered wealthy at that time, I doubt whether anyone crossed the Causeway in any vehicle. Maybe an old bicycle would have served. New bicycles would have been promptly seized by the first soldier you met on the way. He would also grab your watch and fountain pen. Many Japanese soldiers who were peasants had an insatiable passion for watches and fountain pens. It was not unusual for a soldier to sport several watches and fountain pens on his person. These articles were undreamed-of luxuries for him in Japan.

My two friends from Malaya, Chin and Boyle, and I said our thanks and farewells to the hospitable Holmbergs who had sheltered us in the worst of times and shared everything equally with us for a month or more in good heart. As the bus service had not been restored yet, we walked, bags in hand, to the station by way of North Bridge Road. We stopped at High Street when we noticed that the Polar Cafe, a place famous for its ice-cream and curry-puffs, was open. We enjoyed our last curry-puff and ice-cream for the next three and a half years — the tapioca years of privation. We paid pre-war prices with the money we had saved from our pay packets in the Medical Auxiliary Service. Down South Bridge Road, bowing past the sentries at the bridge, we walked through Chinatown and on to the Tanjong Pagar railway station. A huge crowd of men, women and children milled around in confusion with dismay written on their faces at the sight of the open wagons and cattle trucks. They had expected comfortable carriages! A much longer journey awaited us than we imagined as the Japanese engine driver was no respecter of time. He had no timetable to follow. He started and stopped the train at his whim and fancy. At times when he felt like it, he would strip down for a bath at a small station undeterred by the presence of women. It was only when he felt in the mood that he would get the engine moving on its way again. Occasionally when we refugees decided to fill our water-bottles and crowded around the taps, he would get the engine moving, causing a panic and a mad scramble as we rushed back and clambered into the wagons. The train driver clearly was having fun at our expense.

I was one of the more fortunate ones who had the privilege of travelling in a covered truck normally used for transporting animals. One of the three Japanese train guards beckoned me to join him. I do not know why he called me; perhaps he pitied me because I may have been looking forlorn. He was certainly friendly. Later in the train, he took out a photograph of his wife and two children from his wallet and showed it to me. I am sure he missed them, so far away from home on a mission from which he could have hardly expected to return alive. I was surprised at myself for feeling sympathy for an enemy soldier, but I certainly did. Our "conversation" was limited to gesticulations and smiles and odd words in different languages — he in Japanese and me in Malay. Soon we settled down for the night as the train chugged out of Syonan station. I was not to return till October 1945 when the wheel had come full circle and Syonan had become Singapore once more.

We spent two nights on the journey instead of the usual nine hours to reach Kuala Lumpur. In the best of times the train rarely exceeded 30 miles per hour running as it did on a narrow gauge. What with the damage to the rails by bombs, and a part of it having been ripped up during the battles and relaid hastily, and the Japanese fear of sabotage, the train crawled along like a millipede. The capricious behaviour of the driver worsened the delay. The women and children suffered from hunger and thirst. Some of us did what we could to get them drinking water and we distributed some bananas which were offered for sale by a hawker or two on some railway station platforms. Those in the open wagons had to endure the sun and the rain and the coldness of the dawn. But I suppose these physical hardships were bearable for us who had survived the death-dealing bombs and shells. We had survived when so many had perished. We felt as if we were the chosen ones! We had come through the valley of death so the vagaries of the weather were just minor trials to be borne stoically.

The Japanese soldier who befriended me was also bound for Ipoh. My two college friends, Chin and Boyle, continued on their journey to Penang. I said goodbye to them and bowed to the Japanese soldier who shook hands with me. I never saw him again. I managed to contact two friends of mine in Ipoh, Frank Dourado, a medical student, and Kong Hoy Ping, a science student. Both of them were already attempting to earn a living doing business. They had some hilarious experiences in the beginning but developed enough business acumen to do well on the black market. Frank returned to Singapore to complete his medical degree after the war and is now a well-known doctor in Ipoh as well as an authority on orchids. Poor Hoy Ping died of throat cancer soon after the war.

I stayed a couple of days with Frank before leaving on a lorry which was carrying gunny sacks of a very smelly prawn dust fertiliser. I hitched a ride on the stinking sacks for the last 70 miles of my journey home to Cameron Highlands. What a joy it was to be alive and homeward bound!

My mother and younger brother were overjoyed to see me again and were happy to hear that my sister had left early for India, and that I had seen my father in the Cathay Building before he went into internment. He would not have been affected by the march from the Esplanade to Changi because of his long daily walks but little did I realise how close to death he would come before the end of the war. He was a mere skeleton when I saw him again in 1945 in Sime Road internment camp. He had made two wooden shelves and collected old books even in camp!

The mountains and the forests were my home during the three and a half years of the Japanese Occupation. They sheltered me and my family through the days and nights of fear of the Japanese who themselves rarely came our way because they, in turn, feared being ambushed by the guerillas who hid in the forests. The earth yielded us food and the forests afforded us protection and peace from the Japanese while we prayed and waited for deliverance.

My life as a farmer in Cameron Highlands during the Japanese Occupation is a long story — too long to tell you about in this book.

Glossary

alamak	exclamation as in "Oh dear!"
bangsawan	Malay opera
bidan	midwife
bomoh	Malay medicine-man
bubur	rice gruel
cendol	Malay dessert
cupak	a measure of capacity; a measurement for rice
gantang	unit of measure of capacity; 4 cupak = 1 gantang
gilalah	"You are mad!"
ikan kurau	large fish
jambu	a type of fruit; guava or rose-apple
janggut	bearded
kampung	village
Kempetai	Japanese military police
Kora, kora	warning as in "Stop there"

loceng	bell
Maraiyu	Japanese for Malay
musang	civet-cat
nasi padang	rice mixed with fish, egg and vegetables
Orang Asli	aborigine, native
padang	field
parang	a type of large knife
perlahan-lahan	slowly
pelanduk	mouse deer
ronggeng	dance
rotan	rattan cane
sic vita	"Such is life" (Latin)
tuan	"Mr", a title applied to all Europeans
wayang	Chinese opera
yu char kway	deep-fried twisted bread stick

Printed in the United States
By Bookmasters